MENTAL COMBAT

The Sports Psychology Secrets You Can Use to Dominate Any Event!

(Stronger Brain: Stronger Body)

Phil Pierce
Copyright © 2020.

WHAT CAN YOU GET FROM THIS BOOK?

- **Do you know how to "Psych Out" an opponent?**
- *Would you like to learn easy "Mind Hacks" for instant rock-solid confidence and cool?*
- **Want to know how to spot an opponent's personality type (and use it against them)?**
- *Or how to quickly spot deception?*
- **The three tactics for negotiating like a pro**
- *Discover the _____ body position to banish nerves quickly and easily*
- **The truth behind meditation (and why it's easier than you think)**
- *Discover how to unlock the power of your brain for any event*
- **The secret to managing victory...like a winner**
- *The secret to handling defeat ...and coming back stronger*
- **How you can use sports psychology tactics in your daily life (even if you don't do sports!)**
- *And much more!*

The simple aim of this book is to help you unlock the power of your mind, using proven tactics employed by the world's best athletes and sports performers.

Compiled with the input of top Sports Psychologists, Coaches, and Instructors, the secrets of Sports Psychology are out ... and you can start using them right now!

Whether you are a Martial Artist, Boxer, Fitness Fan or just busy at home, in the office or at the gym, you will find powerful tips and techniques to help you boost confidence, increase motivation and banish nerves.

Ever wondered how the pro's do it? Or what secret separates top performers from the rest of us?

Unlock the power of your mind now...

CONTENTS

MENTAL COMBAT   1

What Can You Get From This Book?   2

Mental Combat: How You Can Develop a Stronger Brain (And Body)   7

The Mental Combat Secret (and why managing conflict is so important)   9

What is Sports Psychology Anyway?   14

Why is Sports Psychology Important to Me?   16

Mind Over Matter Over Mind   19

Mind Hacks – Quick Tricks You Can Use Now!   22

Mind Hack No. 1 - Fake It Until You Make It   23

Mind Hack No. 2 – Projecting   26

Mind Hack No. 3 – Power Positions for Instant Confidence   29

6 Proven Tactics to Command Instant Respect   31

PART I

PART ONE: Recognize And Manage The Conflict   39

Quick Eye Training for Lightning Accuracy   43

Exercise: Selective Vision Training   48

Exercise: One-Minute to a Quicker Eye   52

How to Read an Opponent Fast   55

How to Spot a Liar (The 3-Step Secret Code of Deception)   62

Exercise: Learn to Spot a Lie in 3 Minutes   70

Train Your Brain to Handle Adrenaline   72

How to Deal with Panic   75

The Most Powerful Technique for Overall Mental Strength   82

PART II

PART TWO: Analyze And Respond   85

Stand Up for Yourself (The Smart Way)   87

Part 1: How to Get Respect From Your Opponent, Fast   89

Part 2: How to Defend Yourself in a Rising Conflict   93

Personality Types and How You can Overcome Them   97

How You Can 'Psych-Out' an Opponent   102

How to Generate Confidence   107
Three Tricks to Negotiate Like Pro   111
How to Meditate on the Spot   116
How to Meditate in 2 Minutes   117
Improve Your Concentration   121
PRE-EVENT TIPS   125
Pre-Event 1: How to Stay Motivated   128
Pre-Event 2: Train Early   132
Pre Event 3: How to Handle Nerves   135
Pre Event 4: How to Train (Your Mind)   138
Power Words   141
DURING-EVENT TIPS   145
During-Event 1: Handling Adrenaline   146
During-Event 2: Handling Exhaustion   148
POST-EVENT TIPS   151
Post-Event 1: How to Handle Victory   152
Post-Event 2: How to Cope with Defeat   155
Post-Event 3: The "Test" Approach to Defeat   157
Post-Event 4: Speaking after the event   158
Putting it All Together in an Event Plan   160
Applying Mental Combat to Everyday Life   163
Thank You for Reading   167
Ready for More?   168
Self Defence Made Simple   170
How to Meditate in Just 2 Minutes   172

MENTAL COMBAT: HOW YOU CAN DEVELOP A STRONGER BRAIN (AND BODY)

Welcome to Mental Combat, your guide to unlocking the power of your mind and body through simple, proven, psychological techniques that you can use right now.

Whether you are training in a specific style like martial arts, you are an overall fitness and sports enthusiast, or you just want to learn quick tricks to boost confidence and motivation at home or in the office, Mental Combat will provide easy, step-by-step tactics for all of these and more.

The tips and tricks contained within this book have been collected from a variety of expert sources, including top performance coaches, martial arts instructors and a variety of sports psychologists. In compiling this book, I wanted to make sure that the techniques described were not merely hearsay or anecdotes passed from person to person but quantifiable techniques demonstrated, through scientific study, to amplify physical and mental ability.

The typical downside of such research, however, is that the texts can be heavy, technical documents full of difficult jargon and psychological terms. Not so here. I have cherry-picked the very best elements of the scientific studies surrounding sports psychology and present them to you here in a way we can all understand. Plain, simple English with straightforward actionable exercises you can practice to improve your performance. No jargon. No nonsense.

The other important side of mental prowess, of course, is its application beyond sports or martial arts. We go through our daily existence often encountering adversity. Even within the relatively low-conflict environment of an office, we will often encounter others who seek to take opposition or challenge authority in our daily jobs. The right application of mental agility, using specific techniques and tricks, can give you a real edge in your confidence and your demeanor. This will not only help you in your 9-5, but will also give you better prospects in communicating with others, navigating your love life, and finding success on a daily basis.

Over the years, I have been lucky enough to train in a variety of martial arts and fitness styles all around the world, I've written a couple of bestsellers within the fitness and martial arts genres and I've learned from some of the best coaches and instructors around. One of the enduring lessons I've learned is that physical performance is not limited to the muscles and bones of your body. Indeed many of the top performers are physically fit, but they really dominate their opponents from a psychological standpoint. It is these tactics that I want to pass on to you today, so I can help you get the most from your amazing brain.

Ready? Let's go ...

THE MENTAL COMBAT SECRET (AND WHY MANAGING CONFLICT IS SO IMPORTANT)

Life is full of conflict, whether you realize it or not.

Sure, most of us lead fairly peaceful lives on a daily basis but dig a little deeper and it becomes clear that we are surrounded by people in similar positions, all reaching for the same goals. We seek well-paying jobs, nice houses, good health and safety for our families and a long prosperous life. With the world's population exploding to levels never seen before, it's no surprise then that we find ourselves having to "fight" to succeed. This is especially true in sports and combat arts where direct competition is the measure of success.

How you manage this conflict is the key to real success in life.

In nature, an animal typically has two responses: fight or flight. But as humans, we are quite unique in the complexity of our thoughts. This works both for and against us.

Yes, we have developed the incredible intelligence needed to split the atom, examine the human gene code and build worldwide communication networks, but all of this is at the expense of the most powerful and primal instincts of mental strength that our ancestors possessed.

Thousands of years ago, early humans would be faced with death, violence, and threats at every turn. It was a short and dangerous life, but it bred an intrinsic ability to focus on the now, get the job done and go on living.

Today conflict is watered down into so many different forms that the mind has to adapt. Consider the nerves before a sports competition, the pressure before an interview or the way we handle a rival at work or the gym.

We overthink everything. It all seems like life and death ... though ironically nothing is. Our brains are essentially working overtime to filter out all the noise around us. Because of this, we have lost touch with the mindfulness that gives us power.

"Mental Combat" is centered on the idea of managing each conflict and overcoming each challenge through strength of mind and bringing out your inner fighter. This does not involve aggression or anger but simple, intelligent techniques based on Sports Psychology that can "switch on" some of the confidence, motivation, and drive that we all have inside.

I personally come from a martial arts and fitness background, so I'm well aware of the benefits of mental preparation prior to competitions, grading, and tough physical challenges. I have seen extremely talented Black Belts fall to pieces under the pressure of an audience. I've also seen equally nervous youngsters suddenly discover their inner confidence when it's needed and then go on to shine.

Mental Combat is about recognizing the conflict in life, embracing the fact that it is all around us, and using the best tools available to strengthen your mind and, in turn, your body. Mental Combat is not just for sports. Indeed, the concept is useful in overcoming any struggle or stressful scenario we encounter in life.

So while the athletes, martial artists, and sports competitors may find the most benefit from this guide, anyone, from any lifestyle, will be able to use the simple tricks and techniques to improve confidence, overcome stressful situations and unlock the power of their mind.

With that in mind, let's take a look at some of the first steps to take.

How to Begin (The Two-Step Mental Combat Process)

Improving mental ability is always a personal experience and you are encouraged to approach it in whatever way is most comfortable to you. After reading through this guide you may find some techniques resonate more with you than others which is to be expected.

Once you have preferred methods you can incorporate these into your daily life or regular training. But I get it, many people reading this guide will be keen to jump in and have a go at something already. Patience is important, and reading this whole book will offer significantly more benefit than skipping about to find a quick fix, *but* human nature isn't always so patient. So if you want to try something right away, I recommend beginning with the most simple of approaches: Mindfulness (See chapter: *The Most Powerful Technique for Overall Mental Strength*)

Theory is all well and good but let's get straight into the actual process of applying the principles of Mental Combat. The central idea here is all about taking control of any conflict, just like in a self-defense or combat scenario, and not letting the conflict control you. Then we ensure our mind is focused and calm, we assess the opponent or situation and finally, we react with clarity and intelligence.

The actual steps to take are quite simple and this is intentional. In any conflict situation adrenaline and nerves are usually flying around. Sure, there are numerous techniques to manage these (and we will discover these later) but initially, we need the steps to be as simple and memorable as possible.

In fact, the process of managing conflict should eventually become second nature. Only when we have practiced something over and over does it become a natural instinct and this is the ultimate goal.

Each of the following steps will be explored in more detail later but here is a short summary of the process.

.   .   .

The Steps:

1. Recognize the Conflict
2. Manage the Conflict (Be present)
3. Analyze (your opponent or situation)
4. Respond

However, in reality, point 1 and 2 often occur together and applying mental skills in response often occurs together too. So the steps could more accurately be boiled down to:

1. **Recognize and Manage the Conflict**
2. **Analyze and Respond**

Recognize.

The very first step in managing any difficult situation is recognizing it is happening. This may sound obvious and you may think that spotting a conflict is easy but things are not always so straightforward.

Because the stresses of daily life often overwhelm our natural instincts we find ourselves not recognizing the stressors affecting our mind and body all the time. To avoid charging into a situation and reacting purely on emotion we need to take a step back and recognize what is happening.

Manage.

Managing the conflict is all about how we process the events unfolding and control our reaction to them. It is essential that we do not get swallowed by a stressful environment and lose control of our emotions and rational thinking.

Many sports psychology exercises are available to calm the body and mind, giving us an edge over the average untrained person on the street.

Analyze.

Once the body and mind are calm and in control, it is time to take stock of the situation with a clear head. The brain's decision-making process is vastly improved by going through the first two steps of firstly recognizing and then managing the conflict. Now we can use our analytical mind to assess our opponent, calculate weaknesses and strengths and decide our course of action.

Even in cases where there isn't one direct opponent, say, in an important office meeting, analyzing the situation and working out what kind of people you are dealing with can make a massive difference.

Respond.

Finally, we choose to make our move in a deliberate and calculated way. Even during this final stage we constantly feed back into the process, ensuring we recognize what is happening, manage the stress or conflict and analyze the results before responding again.

So what are the best techniques for managing conflict? How can we assess what kind of opponent we are dealing with? And how can we best overcome them? All will be explained, throughout this guide.

The following tips and chapters are broken down into proven Sports Psychology tactics to help you get a real edge in all areas of life and training. These techniques have been grouped into the stages of Mental Combat they best represent; be that managing a conflict, analyzing an opponent or acting upon that information. But before we get to that, let's take a look at why Sports Psychology is so powerful and why we should use it.

WHAT IS SPORTS PSYCHOLOGY ANYWAY?

Most people have a rough concept of Sports Psychology in mind when they hear the term, but few realize the impact it makes in the modern world.

The American Psychological Association's definition of sports psychology refers to the study of how mental or emotional states affect physical performance. In this context, 'sport' refers to any physical performance including, not only athletics but also everything from exercise to running, dance to martial arts. Practical applications of sports psychology utilize psychological concepts to aid sportsmen and women in realizing their greatest potential in these kinds of activities.

When applying sports psychology, you can improve your performance by changing your thoughts. Sports psychology can also be applied to safeguard your health, improve communication skills, foster teamwork, reduce the risk of injury, stimulate rehabilitation and enhance your life.

Most sports psychologists assist coaches or professional athletes. These experts use a wealth of skills and observations. They identify, develop and apply psychological theories to improve physical performance. In order for this training to be effective, they also must be able to diagnose, understand, and eliminate thoughts, responses or habits that interfere with an athlete's ability to perform. Additionally, sports psychologists should seek to ensure that the athlete is able to achieve and maintain enjoyment despite the challenging demands of training and performance.

Not all sports psychologists will approach these responsibilities in the same manner. Those who identify with a social-psychological ideology will spend most of their time manipulating the social environment to engage an athlete's personality. They will work to develop positive interactions between these two factors. On the other hand, a psychophysiological approach would look at processes within the brain and identify how those processes are affecting physical performance. A practitioner who favors a cognitive-behavioral analysis will work with you to see how your internal dialogue is manipulating your physical actions. One psychologist might make use of imagery, meditation or self-talk while another will enlist the use of mini-goals or energy conservation skills.

Basically, whatever works.

Sports psychology is not only practiced by experts, either. Its principles can be applied by individual athletes, coaches, teachers, parents, and personal trainers. There is an ongoing debate in which many players argue what can be labeled sports psychology and who should be able to participate. There are currently no legal restrictions on who may engage its principles, nor are there requirements for specific certifications or licenses to be met. After all, it is difficult to police a science that relies on thought.

Sports psychology is not theoretical gibberish or vague new age talk, though. To the contrary, a recent publication in *Psychology Today* confirms that it is backed by 100 years of concrete science. This mass of research takes an unbiased look at the connections between particular psychological elements and the demands of various physical activities. In addition to being supported by its own professionals and scientists, sports psychology also borrows from a host of related fields including physiology, kinesiology, traditional psychology, and biomechanics.

All of this information converges in an attempt to answer one of two questions. First, how can you use the fundamentals of psychology to optimize your skills and performance? Secondly, in what ways does your involvement in sports and other physical activities influence your mental and physical health both now and in the future?

WHY IS SPORTS PSYCHOLOGY
IMPORTANT TO ME?

There is one thing that all forms of physical competition have in common. The National Center for Biotechnology Information confirms that, regardless of whether you are referring to basketball, ice skating or martial arts, athletic competition generates stress. This creates both psychological and physical symptoms. The physical effects are easy to observe. Your palms get sweaty, your muscles tense up and your heart rate increases. The mental effects can be more difficult to measure. You might begin to doubt your abilities or fear a negative outcome. Many athletes report having difficulty concentrating. This type of psychological stress is called competitive anxiety and it can sabotage all of your physical training.

In order to be successful, your training must involve both physical and psychological skills. By applying sports psychology, you can overcome that inner battle and perform at the top of your abilities. In essence, your mind can be trained to enlist relaxation and concentration in response to competition and stress and this type of training must be in your arsenal if you want to defeat your opponent. Bottom line; sports psychology is essential to breaking down the mental barriers to success.

Sports psychology also stimulates the mental combat attitude needed to conquer stress and sharpen your internal processing. The only way to do this is by determining what thoughts or beliefs are holding you back and replacing them with healthy techniques and philosophies. The benefits of this process are endless.

For starters, it can boost your concentration during your performance while reducing your awareness of the distractions occurring on the sidelines. While most competitors describe being able to focus, all too often that attention is too vague. For example, you might watch your opponent and concentrate on your desire to defeat them without focusing on the position of your hand or the strength of your swing. Sports psychology can provide tips to create a deeper presence in the current moment and awareness of the most immediate obstacles. Instead of doubting your ability to win the match, you instead focus on your ability to assume the correct positions and make accurate movements. This is especially important if you are consistently sabotaging your own performance by expecting to lose.

Research conducted by JM Wikman, for example, demonstrates how sports psychology can be used to teach athletes how to recover from mistakes and conquer the fear of failing. No one is infallible. The thing about training and improving is that you have to make mistakes in order to learn and move forward. You need to have a method of dealing with those errors in such a way that they do not become insurmountable. Martial artists, in particular, must remain calm and focused. It is impossible to adapt in an intense battle if you are too busy beating yourself up over the last move to start planning the next. This shift of focus is particularly valuable when you are recovering from a sports-related injury.

Sports psychology also looks at various forms of motivation and determines which are the most effective. According to American Sports Psychologist Dr. John Bartholomew, successful athletes have to possess a powerful, commanding, internal motivation. In addition to improving your motivation, this can also make your training more effective.

Many sports make use of game plans or strategies which can change at a moment's notice. Sports psychology techniques can help improve the quality and effectiveness of these plans in addition to ensuring your ability to remember them in the heat of the moment. That game plan shouldn't just include physical techniques either. A recent article in the *Journal of Sports Psychology* provides insight into research that shows the importance of having a mental game plan as well.

Paul Lubbers, Ph.D. contends that sports psychology applies not only to sports but also to life off the court. The same skills can be applied to relationships, family, work, future planning, and finances. Consider how often you find yourself frustrated at home or work while still needing to recover and move forward.

Perhaps you have experienced a negative confrontation with a co-worker but needed to stay focused on your goal rather than letting your emotions run wild. Everyone has moments where they need to summon more motivation to push through a long day or quickly find a solution to a problem without being overwhelmed. Having a positive mindset and emotional fortitude can benefit all aspects of your life.

Sports psychology is so important because it combines and considers everything that affects your performance. If you only focus on your physical training, then you won't be able to control all of the factors that contribute to success. Physical training alone will not eliminate stress or conquer your fears. Your muscles will not move without an internal intention to do so.

Use sports psychology to integrate the physical and mental components of your performance. By applying sports psychology, you can adjust your motivation, focus, confidence, energy, memory, and attitude. All of these are powerful tools to help you achieve more than you thought possible.

MIND OVER MATTER OVER MIND

It is easy to think of your mind and your body as two separate parts of your being. In reality, they are mere fibers of the same mesh. Most people are familiar with the concept of "Mind over Matter" but fewer recognize that "Matter over Mind" is equally valid. What does this mean? Simply put, the body and mind are in a constant cycle, each fueling the other. This can either help or hinder its performance.

Mind

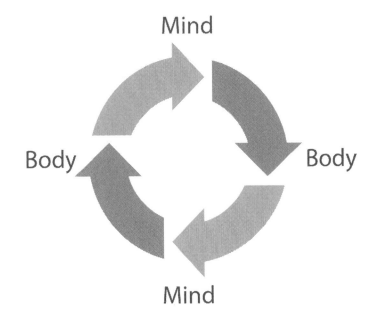

Body   Body

Mind

According to Tim Noakes, MD and *Lore of Running* author, your mind establishes a limit to prevent you from pushing your body past a particular point. This is a safety mechanism to keep you from self-destructing. It also keeps a little extra fuel in your tank so that your body can continue to function after your training session or competitive match. The human body is always capable of doing more. Consider the stories of emergency situations in which an adrenaline rush allows ordinary humans to lift cars or overcome fears.

This self-regulation is generally a good thing. It prevents injury. Unfortunately, the limits set by your mind can sometimes interfere with progress. Imagine how much more you could achieve if you could push beyond that point to rally new personal bests. Science is now showing that it is possible, with training, to push beyond the limit set by your mind. Physical training can teach your mind to let your body move faster and use more strength. This type of training has to be done carefully and gradually to prevent injury, but it can be done.

In the past, it was believed that once an animal learned to fear something, the memory of that fear would never leave. New studies conducted by Kevin Corcoran at the University of Puerto Rico for example, are now blasting through that old way of thinking. These studies show that it is possible to overcome old fears or mental limits with mental conditioning that covers those blocks with positive memories. This is because new experiences are recorded in your prefrontal cortex, which overrules the amygdala, where those primal fears are stored. Your mind can be taught to overcome any limitations.

Your mindset also radically affects your motivation levels. Visualizing the end goal and staying mindful of the tasks at hand can be important tools in staying on track. This is an example of mind over matter. However, you might sometimes be reluctant to start your training session because you are mentally tired or stressed. In this case, matter over mind is just as important. When you jump in anyway, physical exercise stimulates the release of feel-good endorphins which boost your mood. When you are in a better mood, you will experience a greater sense of motivation to keep you moving forward.

What this means is that mental preparation is important, but a healthy diet and exercise program is also necessary to nourish a powerful body. Your body and mind both need to be in top condition if you want to fight at your best. While this guide is primarily focused on sharpening your mind and removing mental blocks, you cannot ignore your body altogether. Train both aspects together.

MIND HACKS – QUICK TRICKS YOU CAN USE NOW!

While a deeper understanding of psychology is important if you wish to master Mental Combat, many people will read a guide like this for quick tricks or techniques that they can use now – not after reading chapters of information. There is nothing wrong with this of course. We live in an age of instant gratification and so we are encouraged to seek out the fastest result.

Yes, you will get better results from reading this whole book, and I implore you to do so. But, if you want some quick 'tricks' that you can use for a fast boost to your performance, then the following "Mind Hacks" are psychologically proven techniques that work almost instantly and require almost no understanding (even if the methodology is fascinating).

MIND HACK NO. 1 - FAKE IT UNTIL YOU MAKE IT

I wanted to begin these quick "Mind Hacks" with a trick that has been used by movie stars, world leaders and politicians for years. In fact, this technique is so powerful that you can try it right now and see results in seconds.

Have you ever met someone you considered confident and relaxed and wondered how they managed to be so composed? The real secret to beating stress and taking control of your mind is to accept that no one is born immune to stress. We all experience it. We all have the choice of how to handle it. Those who appear unfazed by tense situations start by simply "acting" unfazed until it ultimately becomes a reality.

Most of us know someone who lives by the **"fake it until you make it"** philosophy. Psychology has a different term for it—status-enhancement theory —but it all amounts to the same outcome. By acting dominant and confident, you give others the impression that you are skilled, and you also project that confidence to yourself. By acting as though you are mentally tough, you actually succeed in being tough.

We already know that the mind has a powerful control over the body, but did you know that the brain can have difficulty separating the way you behave from the way you think? You can use this principle of *acting calm to become calm* to establish long-term benefits for your mind and body by emulating the mannerisms of confident and relaxed people.

The more often you "fake it" (act in the way you would like to feel), the more often the brain begins to change and accept this change as agreeable. The more times your brain accepts this change, the more permanent the effects become. Eventually, they will take a fixed place in your personality.

For example, every time you feel stressed, take a moment to breathe deeply and imagine yourself being calm and confident. Begin doing this once or twice a day, but continue until you reach four, five, or six times a day. One day you will wake up and realize that you now ARE calm most of the time and with that has come the natural confidence.

It has even been shown that mentally imagining someone fictional, with a confident demeanor, and trying to emulate that person can have similar benefits. If a situation starts to create stress and discomfort, imagine what your confident fictional hero might do.

How would James Bond react?

What would that confident President or Politician do?

How would that popular movie star respond?

It may sound odd, but these mental exercises have been shown to stimulate confidence. From confidence comes relaxation and positive action.

Let's say for example, that you need a boost in energy or motivation. You could spend hours beating yourself up for that lack of drive, or you could simply 'fool' yourself into believing you are the kind of person filled with motivation already. Simply close your eyes and focus on exactly what that kind of person would behave like, then just emulate that. You don't have to believe it or be an expert you just need to copy the behavior of your ideal self.

MIND HACK NO. 2 – PROJECTING

"Projecting" nicely follows "Fake it until you make it". In essence, these are the quick, physical techniques you can use right now to trick your mind into feeling more confident and relaxed – even if it isn't. Projecting is a way of extending an expression of confidence outward.

Remember that the more you adopt these types of techniques, the more they become second nature and allow you to handle the challenges in everyday life.

Whether you are entering an important meeting, a competitive sports match or simply meeting someone for the first time, sometimes we need a quick boost of charisma, energy, and charm to portray our best self.

The following physical actions can be used right now to project a more confident and relaxed persona. Consider practicing each, the next time you encounter someone new.

Projecting with Posture

You may assume people look at your face first, but research shows that it's often a person's posture or stature we notice first. Create a confident stance and half of the battle is already won.

- Stand up or sit up a little straighter. Imagine a thread is pulling the top of your head to the sky.
- Consciously drop your shoulders a little and ease them back, gently pushing the chest forwards slightly.
- Tuck your head back and make sure it sits on top of your neck – not protruding forward
- Stay relaxed and keep the shoulder low and the chest steady as you breathe.

Projecting with Voice

Our voice is the primary tool for communication and beyond body language becomes one of the most powerful tools we have. As such it can make or break an interaction.

- The next time someone speaks to you, lower the tone of your voice slightly when you respond. (This is especially true on phones, where the electronic signal can raise tone). This creates depth and authority.
- Speak slightly slower. Approximately 80% of your normal speed. This should still sound natural, but convey an air of purposeful speech.
- Don't use um, or erms to fill the gap. This one can be tricky to

learn since we use them so often. But instead of these nothing filler-words, either take a moment of silence and then respond, or use something more intentional, starting a response with "So," or "Well."

Projecting in Person

After your stature and voice have been adjusted to project the most confidence, there are additional subtle opportunities throughout interactions with others to assert yourself and immediately create a more confident you.

- If someone asks you a question in an important environment, take two whole seconds before responding. Count these in your head as you show that you are thinking about it. This demonstrates that you are not simply responding by blurting out any old answer, but in control of your mind and body and adds weight to your responses.
- Breathe as soon as you become aware of stress taking control. Now focus on that breath for four seconds inhaling, four holding, and four exhaling. Once more, this demonstrates your ability to be cool under pressure.
- Maintain relaxed eye contact during interactions. It's not a staring contest and you don't have to look at them the whole time, but keeping your gaze steadily fixed on the person you are interacting with shows them that you are fully engaged in the conversation and asserts a level of dominance from the outset.

As a set of quick tips to help you emulate confidence, these tricks not only work but actually build long-term relaxation through assurance and repetition. Give them a go!

MIND HACK NO.3 – POWER POSITIONS FOR INSTANT CONFIDENCE

We have already mentioned how a quick change of posture can stimulate confidence and relaxation. Did you know that certain, specific body positions literally generate a confidence-boosting hormone?

Testosterone is the hormone most commonly associated with aggression and strength, but in stressful situations, it can serve a great advantage. A surge of testosterone will bolster your nerves, allowing you to act more relaxed and assertive. Assertiveness is a common characteristic of confident people

Not surprisingly, research from Harvard University has now confirmed that increased testosterone levels can boost your confidence. Whereas, reduced testosterone can lead to anxiety.

Power Positions

One symbol of confidence is the body taking up more space or expanding its width. You can see this all throughout nature. A frightened animal will curl up in a ball or make itself small, whereas a confident predator will stretch itself out, taking up space in a relaxed manner. Research shows that by assuming these positions we actually generate confidence boosting chemicals on the spot.

Use the quick strategy below to instantly summon more testosterone and, in turn, improve your response to stress.

- **Stand tall with your hands on your hips in a confident pose for 1-2 minutes.** Once again, imagine a piece of string is drawing your head towards the sky and keep your back straight while your hands rest on your hips.

Or,

- **Sit or stand with your hands positioned behind your head with your elbows pointed out and upward for 1-2 minutes.** Again sit or stand nice and straight but this time lace or hold the hands behind the head in your best "hammock on the beach" pose.

Incredibly, studies have shown that both of these body positions can boost your testosterone, and therefore your confidence, by as much as 20% in just 2 minutes. One of these studies from the University of Oregon also detected a simultaneous decrease in cortisol, the hormone associated with stress and nerves. A win-win situation.

Enlist one of these positions immediately before a big meeting or competitive event. Practice for two minutes every day for a regular testosterone boost. Try it right now. You should feel more confident in a matter of seconds.

6 PROVEN TACTICS TO COMMAND INSTANT RESPECT

Attract Instant Respect by Applying Psychology-Based Strategies

Before we get into the main part of addressing conflict I wanted to explore another option. That is the process of avoiding the conflict altogether by simply being the kind of confident, driven person that others respect.

Gaining the respect of your peers is essential in every facet of life, especially in a competitive environment. When someone respects you, they accept you as a person and value what you have to offer. Typically, acquiring respect would require a lengthy process of proving oneself. You might gradually demonstrate your good character by consistently acting with honesty and integrity.

But what about those times when you need to gain someone's respect quickly? For example, you might only have a short conversation in which to gain the respect of a potential employer, an important customer, or your future in-laws. Below, I've devised a list of powerful psychology-based strategies you can apply to attract respect instantly. You'll still want to put in the effort to develop and maintain good character, but these steps can definitely speed up the process.

1. **Guard Your Time**

This strategy is first on the list because as a society we have become a little self-absorbed. As such, disrespecting one another's time has become common-place. Think about how often friends, dates, or work colleagues just show up late and offer little in the way of excuse. Simply shrugging as if it's the most normal thing in the world. Well, it shouldn't be.

The fact is, when someone doesn't respect you, they don't respect your time. They show up early or more likely late, over and over, they forget to call when they say they would, or they insist you rush over to help them with little warning. Why? Because they are subconsciously asserting themselves over you and your needs. They have decided that you don't matter as much as them.

When people behave this way, they are demonstrating that their time is more important than yours and often demonstrating that they never even gave your time a second thought. It's not only selfish behavior from them, but submissive behavior from you.

The flip side is that by protecting your personal time, you can instantly elicit immediate respect. This is particularly crucial in relationships and also in friendships and even at work, where technology is now allowing employers to invade personal time with text messages and emails.

Don't stand for it. You are worth more than that.

Rules for guarding your time.

- Don't allow yourself to always be available. You have a life and others should respect that.
- Don't be afraid to say no. Help out when and if you want to. Don't feel obliged.
- Never sit around waiting for a phone call—use your time.
- Call out friends/family on their behavior if they are always late. Politely but firmly tell them it is unfair.
- Allow yourself downtime. This is a time for yourself. No one should intrude.

You should respect others enough to accept that life sometimes gets in the way. But at the same time, don't give them a free pass. If someone arrives late or misses an appointment a couple of times, bring it up before it becomes a habit. Calmly mention that while you understand how busy they are, you are busy too. Let them know that your time is valuable and that, in the future, you'd appreciate a quick call or message to advise that they are running late. This way you neither of you will end up wasting your time. More importantly, you are communicating that your time is important, and this will generate respect.

2. Take A Pause

Often when we enter a room, we hurry. This is especially true when we are preparing to be interviewed or give a presentation in front of an audience. If you are nervous, there is a tendency to feel rushed. However, by diving right in you are actually giving away your power. In essence, you are demonstrating once again, that their time is more important than yours, and so you hurry along not to waste the opportunity.

Switch the script. Take as much time as you need to compose yourself. Slow down and take a pause, even an animated one.

- Take a look at your audience, and acknowledge their presence. Smile.
- Though it might seem like an eternity when you are standing center stage, take that last deep breath. It only uses a few seconds. In that time, you establish anticipation. This is one key to instant respect.
- While they have been waiting you have become their sole focus and created a commanding presence. Now they are ready to really listen to what you have to say or do. You can use this same strategy in personal interactions as well.

3. Use Body Language to Command Space

We sometimes subconsciously reduce the way others perceive our worth by making ourselves physically small. If you are uncertain or uncomfortable, you might feel as though you are invading the other person's space, and so you try to be as unobtrusive as possible. You stand in one spot near the corner during the entire party with your arms crossed close to your body. During the presentation you stand directly behind the podium, clutching your notes. This is the opposite of what you should do in competition, presentations or group interactions where you want to attract respect or even acceptance.

- Instead, try gesticulating away from your body. Use your arms a little to open a space in front.
- Use your palms face up and don't cross your limbs in front of your body
- Roll your shoulders back a touch and take deeper breaths, to inflate your chest.
- Instead of standing still, move around. You can even pace a little.

The more open you are with your body language and your confidence to move about, the more you demonstrate your desire to be seen and heard. Your presence is every bit as valid as anyone else's so let it be known. Using your body language to command the space is the second strategy to instantly attract attention and respect.

4. End Every Sentence as Confidently as You Begin

Do you ever catch yourself mumbling, or trailing off at the end of a sentence when you misplace your train of thought? What if I told you that how you speak is far more important than what you actually say? Trailing off shows your companion that you weren't sure of yourself. When you display this lack of confidence, you lose respect.

Here's another example. Do you stop speaking the second someone interrupts you?

- Don't let anyone run over you with their words. In any type of gathering it is common for people to talk over one another at times, but in competitive situations, it is important to have a strategy you can stick to.
- Complete your sentence, repeating the parts spoken over if needed.
- Then give the floor to the other party. By doing this, you demonstrate that you value your own thoughts and you also hint that they should respect what you have to say too.
- Let them speak and have their say. Respect works both ways.

5. Put on A Brave Face

Do you remember the old adage "fake it until you make it?" This phrase has stood the test of time because it's true and we explore it more elsewhere in this guide. Most people are timid in social circumstances. However, I'll let you in on a little secret. Nothing bad is going to happen if you manage to find the confidence to step up and break the ice. In fact, there's probably a lot of other people in the room who wish they had your confidence. Even if it doesn't come naturally, fake it to start.

- Put on your game face and go introduce yourself to that person across the room. Actually, introduce yourself to everyone and make the rounds.
- This can be even more effective if the person is a rival or another competitor. Good sporting attitude can make you appear incredibly confident. As if you are so good, you have no rivals.
- Networking is powerful so don't let a little shyness keep you sitting in the corner waiting to be called on.
- Make some friends. You can even take your brazenness a step further by introducing a few of your new friends to one another. Not only will they appreciate that you took the initiative (so they didn't have to) but they will respect you for it and find you that much more interesting. So, put on a brave face and stop waiting for them to come to you.

6. Stop Letting Bad Behavior Slide

Just like letting people get away with being late all the time, when you allow other bad behavior to slide, you tell people it's fine that they don't respect you or the rest of your peers. Stop allowing disrespect to be the status quo.

- Call people out on their poor behavior. When someone does or says something that is uncalled for, make it known and ask them to stop.
- This includes when the disrespect comes from someone who has implied superiority. Teachers, parents, bosses. No-one is immune. They may be shocked at first. However, in the end, they'll respect you even more for having the courage to call them out—kindly.
- Call people out with calm confidence and reason. Shouting and ranting will only lose you respect long term.

Displaying the confidence to hold people to a higher standard in life will earn their respect—even if it is uncomfortable and makes them upset in the moment. It will also earn you the respect of others nearby. Keep demonstrating your good character and encourage the same behavior from your peers. Push them to do better and they'll respect you for it.

Applying What You Learned

I hope you've found these six strategies enlightening. Although they are very quick tactics, they truly do work and can make a big difference in your life. Use them to attract instant respect.

Going forward, you'll know exactly what to do to quickly gain the respect of your peers. Can you already think of someone who doesn't respect your time or decisions? Which strategy will you apply to change their perception? Remember that these methods are about developing mutual understanding and helping other people to recognize your right to be heard, seen and listened to. Extend the benefits by continuing to display honesty and integrity and, most importantly, returning that same respect to others.

PART ONE: RECOGNIZE AND MANAGE THE CONFLICT

As we have previously discussed, recognizing a conflict is the first step to taking control and turning things to your advantage. The management and processing of stressful events in your mind is the second stage.

Recognizing Conflict

It can be difficult to spot an escalating situation which may turn into a conflict, simply because we live such sedentary lifestyles.

Sure, in a competition or a sparring match, the opponent is obvious and a clash of abilities (or fists) is to be expected. But what about the less obvious scenarios, where a work colleague or friend is acting unusually? What about those situations where we don't even notice someone trying to manipulate us until it's too late, how do we handle those?

The following chapters will explore the process of identifying conflict through understanding people and how they operate. This includes spotting deception, reading people's intentions and understanding elements of body language and vocal codes. Following this, we will take a look at methods for handling the conflict, how to address your response and perhaps most importantly, how to handle stress.

But first, I wanted to address a common misconception about stress, and why it can actually help more than you think.

The Stress Myth

You've probably heard those dubious statistics thrown around. "Stress is the cause of 80% of illness." "Stress causes X disease." "Stress makes you fat." Etc etc.

Most of it is nonsense. Yes, chronic stress *can* have serious negative consequences in life, but not all stress is bad. In fact, the acute raised pulse we often experience is essential in preparing our bodies for action and is essential in a competitive environment. It can also help us escape a bad situation or become physically stronger and more resistant to fatigue for a while.

However, at what point does this kick in? And when does it stop working to our benefit and start making things more difficult?

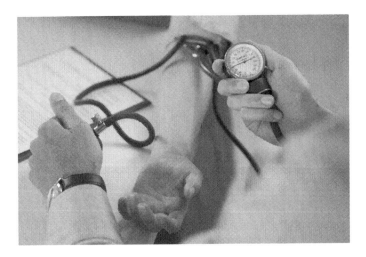

A principle known as the "Inverted U Hypothesis" has long been used as a tool for measuring performance vs. pulse. Sports coaches and psychologists discovered that at a certain point our increased heart rate helps our cognitive functions and large physical actions the most. After this point, things start to break down quickly.

The following looks at how our pulse rate affects bodily functions.

Over 115 Beats Per Minute – Fine Motor Skills like texting on a phone or writing something becomes more difficult

115 – 145 BPM - Complex Motor Skills like throwing an object or aiming at something using larger muscle movements hit their peak.

Over 145 BPM – The previous Complex Motor Skills start to break down, but Gross Motor Skills like running or tasks using the whole body remain at peak levels.

Over 175BPM – Everything starts to break down. Physical and mental abilities deteriorate across the board.

The thing to take from this is that if you feel overwhelmed when under stress, it is perfectly normal. You shouldn't be alarmed. In fact, the elevated heart rate could prove essential to help you achieve your goals. If, however, you find yourself facing the challenge of an ever-increasing heart rate and a lack of control plus incoming panic symptoms there are some simple steps to take. We will explore these in the following chapters.

QUICK EYE TRAINING FOR LIGHTNING ACCURACY

Have you ever watched those old western movies where the two gunslingers meet at noon and duel it out to see who has the fastest draw? Remember how they seemed lightning fast on the reflexes?

While we may not live in an age of duels at noon (and indeed there is some debate as to whether they even happened as depicted in the old west) the speed your eyes can take in information and translate that into usable signals for your muscles, is still very much a helpful skill in the modern world. The ability to see, analyze and react fast and hopefully faster than your opponent is a critical talent to give you the edge over completion in life.

This chapter will share Sports Psychology research demonstrating why including Quick Eye Training in your Mental Combat conditioning is not just a great idea, but essential to your overall performance in life. At the end we will look at a couple of exercises you can use to program your mind and body to improve your quick vision and create smooth, synchronous movements.

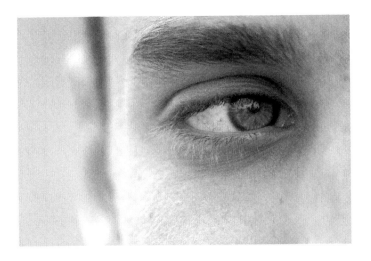

But what is vision anyway?

On a technical level, vision refers to the process the human body uses to see and perceive its environment through data presented in the form of light. You may assume that since your eyesight is ok, there is nothing to improve, but your ability to quickly see and respond to everything happening in your environment is affected by more than just the visual acuity score measured by your eye doctor.

The ability to discern people, objects, threats, and dangers quickly, especially when they are in motion, relies on smooth communication with your mind, allowing more time for mental processing, decision making, and action.

The difference can be split-seconds. Split-seconds can be life and death.

Improving Accuracy with Improved Vision?

In order to better understand how Quick Eye Training could improve your accuracy, it is important to understand how vision really works. Despite what many people assume, vision is not limited to the eyes, though it does start there. To be more specific, vision begins with your cornea and crystalline lens. These direct light toward the retina, situated at the back of your eye. How well you see depends on how well your brain perceives this light. As the light is focused on the retina, neural signals are sent toward the visual cortex along what is known as the visual pathway.

The visual cortex is in the back of your brain, inside of the occipital lobe.

This is where you process visual information from each eye and combine that information to form one complete picture. This information is then sent along your brain's communication network so the information can be translated into a perception of your environment. Mental Combat Training techniques, such as Quick Eye Training, can aid this process in occurring more quickly.

You may be wondering why this is important, especially if you've never noticed any visual shortcomings. The answer is that quick, accurate coordination relies heavily on this communication between your brain and your eyes. You need more than visual acuity to smoothly catch an object, improve your aim, know exactly when to strike, or quickly determine how to adjust your body to maintain balance while absorbing a blow. It helps with all those unexpected moments outside of sports as well. For example, grabbing and righting that glass of wine before it tumbles off the edge of the table and stains the carpet. Or, catching hold of your child or spouse when they begin to trip— saving them from potential injury. Or even, safeguarding against personal injury yourself by avoiding accidents on the roadway or around say, a swimming pool, or high ledge.

Essentials of Coordination

Eye-hand coordination is a complicated function requiring lots of brain and body regions to work in unison. Practice is essential to uniting your visual and motor skills more seamlessly. This is essential for healthy child development and academic success in addition to completing the countless daily tasks that call upon us as adults, both in real life and in the world of competition.

Coordination is one of the most fundamental attributes of good performance in conflict and in life. Good coordination between the eyes and the brain allow you to perform movements with greater complexity, more quickly, more smoothly, and with greater confidence. Psychotherapist and personal trainer Natalie Wise contends that there is a "definite link between good coordination skills and confidence. When you are comfortable with your body and know its strength and abilities, this comes through in your confidence."

You train the rest of your body for improved performance, so why not your eyes? It is interesting to note that despite the importance of eyesight and perception in staying safe and completing everyday tasks, it is one of the most overlooked skills we possess. It is not difficult to train your eyes to work more quickly and improve your accuracy for optimum performance.

Establishing dynamic visual acuity may allow you to see objects in motion more quickly and more clearly. This is different from the 20/20 vision you might already experience while you and your target are both sitting still. Life is in constant motion and so it is important to train your eyes and brain to work quickly while in motion too. Then you will be better able to use your body to carry out actions based on the information your brain is receiving from your eyes.

Benefits of Quick Eye Training

- Hardwires your brain for complex movement
- Greater accuracy and aim
- Cut training time by improving efficiency
- Develop faster reaction times
- Predict where injuries might occur and prevent them
- Improve self-awareness and self-perception
- Freedom to confidently explore more complicated activities

Applying Sports Psychology To Vision Theories

Sports psychologists constantly seek to discover techniques and ways of thinking that enable us to push the limits of what can be achieved in terms of both performance and human experience, and the research shows that Quick Eye Training can help. As early as 1969, H. T. A. Whiting was able to distinguish, through a series of tests involving the processing of input, decision-making, and output, that the eyes register stimulus information from the environment and transmit it to the brain. However, he found that the amount of information available at any one time is too great to process consciously at any time. As such, your brain develops a *selective transmission of information*.

Through repetitive use of Quick Eye Training, you can retrain your eyes and your brain to focus on specific information relevant to the task at hand. A psychophysiology study conducted in 2012 found this to be especially true for young golfers. The group that experienced eye training showed better performance results compared to those who had solely been coached on their swinging techniques (Moore et al, 2012). In 1996, a study by Worrel concluded that baseball players who underwent visual training showed significant performance improvement. Similar results were observed in a study involving Hockey players (Calder, 1998). While good techniques and solid coaching are important, they alone cannot replace the benefits of improved coordination from eye training. Quick vision really does make a difference.

It's not surprising then that the athletes whom we consider highly skilled typically demonstrate better visual abilities than your average individual (Ophthlamol, 1996). Thankfully, visual training can significantly improve anyone's sports performance.

Improving Visual Limitations Through Specific Eye Movements

There are several different types of eye movements that are applied to observing and tracking objects in motion. For example, saccadic eye movements scan a field rapidly, whereas vestibulo-ocular movements incorporate head motion with eye focus while also aiding balance. Additionally, a motion known as vergence eye movement is essential to focus at varying distances.

Smooth pursuit eye movements may provide the most detailed information about an object's movement. However, this type of eye movement is most effective at tracking slow-moving objects. The slower the object is, the more smoothly you'll be able to track it. Since many things move quickly, you'll need to hone this ability, as well as vergence eye movements in order to track various objects in various locations, ideally simultaneously.

Eye movements and purpose

- Saccadic - *Scans rapidly*
- Vestibulo-ocular - *Coordinates with head movements/balance*
- Vergence - *Views varied distances*
- Smooth Pursuit - *Tracks slow-moving objects*

Don't worry too much about learning these terms. They can be helpful in understanding the different ways our eyes process data around us, but ultimately they don't help us physically improve our eye to brain ability.

EXERCISE: SELECTIVE VISION TRAINING

Here's a quick exercise to demonstrate the benefits of quick vision and how to apply mental processing to quickly remove extraneous details.

Next time you are on the street, watch a car driving past you. Don't spot it off in the distance and watch it approach, and don't follow it down the street. Simply observe as a car enters and exits your field of vision in a normal manner.

The car should be driving at full, regular speed and ideally, it should be a vehicle you aren't familiar with.

Easy:
What color was it?
What type of car was it? Small, family, mini-van etc?

Intermediate:
How many people were inside?
What color were the wheels

Challenging:

What make and model was it?

What color were the seats inside?

To gather all of this information is incredibly difficult and even if you think you have all the answers, many times our brains are simply making educated guesses based on experience. Let's try the same exercise again.

Once more, observe a car passing, but this time, focus on only two things:

What color are the wheels?

How many people are inside?

Easier right? It may sound obvious, but it can be difficult to maintain a constant focus on things that are either close to you or moving quickly. This problem is multiplied when we are under pressure and suffering the effects of stress.

The key to overcoming these limitations is to be more selective in the information we seek. As mentioned previously, the mind can be trained to focus visual attention on specific aspects to compensate for not being able to observe such a large volume of information quickly. For example, instead of trying to observe all of an opponent's hand, foot, and head movements, you might focus on one or two critical features. IE The useful stuff.

You can then use saccadic, or scanning, eye movements to observe the most essential components.

An earlier example described a scenario where a glass of wine is about to spill. Trying to observe the tablecloth, what is on the table, the color of the carpet, how full the glass is, and the expressions of the guests all at once--is too much information for your mind to process and form a fast reaction. Instead, focus on one thing. The distance between your hand and the stem of the glass. This will result in a quicker, more accurate response.

Turn Your Eyes On

Another large component of visual training is practicing active, mindful watching. Have you ever found yourself zoning out in a restaurant? Suddenly you become aware that there is a stranger across the room looking at you suspiciously. You didn't mean to stare. In fact, you might be especially embarrassed because you were previously unaware of your own behavior. You were looking at them, but you weren't really. Your eyes were open, but they were essentially turned off.

Sometimes we don't see things that are right in front of our face. Sometimes it happens because we are "zoning out" and other times there is just a lapse in our visual tracking. It becomes worse as we age, though regular practice and training can reduce and even reverse this trend.

Blinking, bizarrely enough, is another problem. Now I'm not suggesting you stop blinking. But you blink approximately 25 times every minute. Even though your eyes are only closed for approximately $1/10^{th}$ of a second, you still might miss an important detail (Riggs, & Moore, 1980), particularly during a competitive event where actions happen fast. Anxiety can aggravate the gaps by making you blink more often. Though it might seem hard to miss something that is happening so close, it happens more than you'd think. Especially in a fast-paced environment where seconds really count.

Examples
Fastball

Take a fastball pitched in Baseball. The ball may be delivered at up to 100mph. That means the ball is traveling at approximately 45m per second. (Although it may not travel that far.)

This means a blink of $1/10^{th}$ of a second misses a potential 4 meters of travel. This can literally be the difference between a hit and a miss.

Punch

Imagine a competition or in the worst case, a dangerous self-defense scenario. An opponent throws a strike toward your face. Now punches can be fast our slow, but a typical punch from a fully grown, reasonably strong adult can be delivered at 25-30 mph, which doesn't sound like much ... until you are hit by it. At a conservative 25mph, the fist is traveling 11 meters per second. Let's be even more conservative and say 10m/s.

A blink, in this case, would miss a full one meter of arm movement. Just for reference, that is about the same as your nose to your fingertip. In other words, a full-length punch. The reason we normally don't miss them completely is because:

1. We blink either half way before or after the punch
2. Or we see the persons overall body movement, indicating the strike incoming

Sports Vision

So $1/10^{th}$ of a second may not sound like much, but in many cases we are often talking about events that occur in milliseconds, meaning every nanosecond counts when it comes to perceiving what is happening and how to react.

This has actually given birth to a new area of sports science research. Termed *Sports Vision*, the new field melds sports psychology with motor learning, vision science, and neuroanatomy. Each of these can offer information on the way we see and perceive, and how we can improve our performance by improving our vision while in motion.

Fortunately, we have found that the brain and the eyes often work together to detect movements faster than the individual components. Though it is impossible to consistently track the movement of a fast-moving object, your brain is pretty good at predicting where it might end up. With practice, you can train your brain to make these predictions more quickly and more accurately. This can make a huge difference in your reaction time whether during competition or just in life in general. A faster response time of even just a few seconds can save your life in some scenarios.

By practicing Quick Eye Training, you can learn how to focus your visual attention on the most essential cues. This means your perception of your environment will become more efficient and you will be able to make better, more educated decisions and reactions. You'll know exactly when to block, and when to initiate your offense.

EXERCISE: ONE-MINUTE TO A QUICKER EYE

Within each of your eyes, there are six extraocular muscles that control direction. Their job is to make sure that your vision can be redirected to observe objects of interest with excellent clarity. Close study reveals that top athletes tend to utilize very specific and especially efficient eye movement strategies for this, allowing them to focus their attention on the most important areas.

It also allows them to track and predict the moment of objects within their visual field while they are still in motion. As a result, they are better able to predict what they need to do next and direct their own reactions with far greater success and accuracy. Practicing switching focus, through this simple eye exercise, will allow you to build towards high-speed movements and faster reaction times, too.

Step 1: Select two similar items from around your home or gym. For example, two weights or plates. Ideally, these should be approximately the same size and shape. Place these objects on the floor in front of you. Place one object 2 feet away and the other 8 feet away. These measurements need not be exact, but use this approximation as a guide.

Step 2: Now stand two feet away from the closest object and focus all of your attention on that location. Stare at it for about 20 seconds. While you do this, try to observe as many details as you can, the smaller and more specific the better.

Step 3: Next, quickly shift your attention to the object that is 8 feet away. Focus on it for 20 seconds, while also trying to observe a great amount of detail.

Step 4: Continue alternating back and forth between the two objects for one minute.

Engaging different focal ranges quickly is a great way to train your eyes for long term benefits in everything from sports and fitness to reading people at a distance and even driving. With so much of our lives spent staring at a computer screen, our eyes can become fatigued and suffer reduced effectiveness at different sight ranges. This exercise is one way to counter this and build visual acuity.

Want to take it further?

1. Repeat the exercise above, but instead of weights or household objects, use a paperback book, or magazine.
2. Place each one at different focal length. Say, two feet and 10 feet on the floor.
3. Turn your back to them.
4. Start a timer for five seconds.
5. Now quickly turn and look between the two covers. You must assimilate as much detail about them as possible.
6. When five seconds is up. Turn back around and grab a notepad.
7. Now you must jot down as much detail as you can about each cover.
8. What was the main story about? What colors are on the cover? Who is the author? Or, if you are feeling creative, try to sketch out a mock-up of the cover.
9. Finally, turn back and compare what you jotted down against what is there?
10. How did you do?

Once you have some practice under your belt, you might want to try increasing the intensity. Repeat the exercise, this time focusing on each object for just 3 seconds each. It may help to set a repeating timer so you can focus all of your vision on the object rather than the clock. Finally, for a big challenge, try the exercise again with 2-second intervals.

This Quick Eye Training Exercise can help you reduce your reaction time and accuracy by training your mind to adjust your visual focus more quickly. Repeat this activity often. Once you feel like you have mastered this technique, you can mix it up by incorporating more objects or alternating the distances between them.

The Big Takeaway

The research shows that quick vision is essential to daily living, and exercises that improve visual skills can have a big impact. The best news is that Quick Eye Training doesn't have to be extensive or time-consuming. In fact, most report significant improvement after adding just a few minutes of training to their normal routine. To improve your coordination, perception, reaction time, and accuracy you really only need a few minutes a day. You can even multiply the benefits by integrating visual training into your regular daily activities as well.

HOW TO READ AN OPPONENT FAST

Use Psychology Cues to Read People with Incredible Accuracy

Have you ever been in a conversation and wished you knew what the other person was thinking? Ever wondered if what a person says is really what they mean?

Being able to use psychology to read people is an amazing ability that has so many applications, both within and outside of a competitive or combat situation. The skill to take a quick look at a person and instantly have a rough idea of their intentions is not only powerful but could be the difference between winning and losing a match-up when the chips are down.

Just think how much easier things would be if you automatically knew what someone was thinking or feeling. You'd be able to calm their concerns or answer their questions in a flash. Plus, you'll save a ton of energy and frustration by knowing when it's time to back off, change your approach or move along altogether. Even more importantly, by reading people's raw reactions, you'll get unfiltered feedback that will allow you to quickly identify where you need to make adjustments in your own approach. This kind of feedback is simply impossible to attain under normal circumstances.

Below you will find a simple, highly effective six-step strategy that will enable you to do just that, and with incredible accuracy too.

Ready? Let's go.

1. Develop Greater Awareness of Yourself

It all starts from within. You can't expect to understand other people unless you first understand yourself. Every human is unique, but we are also surprisingly similar in the way we express emotions and make judgments. That means you can get better at reading other people simply by reading yourself more closely.

If you are self-aware, you will be able to notice the way your opinions of others are formed. Keep in mind that most people develop a strong opinion of a new acquaintance within a few minutes. Those opinions can change or grow based on subtle cues from the other person's tone, posture, or statements. Get in touch with your own cues, and then you'll know what cues alter the way people perceive you as well.

- Take a minute to look in the mirror, notice how you appear when you are relaxed, calm.
- Next, think about a time in your life when you experienced extreme stress. Close your eyes and really put yourself back in that moment. Then, quickly open your eyes and take another look. What has changed?
- Consider your face, any tension in your shoulders and posture
- Ask friends and family about any mannerisms or 'tells' you have. Ask them to be honest.

2. Determine If You Have Someone's Attention

This might be one of the easiest aspects of reading someone. Have you ever been talking and then suddenly found yourself wondering if the other person is even listening? Or do you sometimes wonder if an opponent is even aware of you? Locate where their attention is focused and you will have a pretty good idea if they are engaged in what you are saying at all.

The first biggest clue will be where their eyes are focused. Remember, eye contact is huge when you are trying to forge a connection and exude confidence. Is your companion looking you in the eye, or have they focused away?

Another clue is the direction of their body. Are they turned towards you, or away? The chest region, in particular, is typically turned toward an area of focus or interest. Body language and focus are the two biggest indicators of whether your listener is actively engaged.

The third clue is their participation in the conversation if one is underway, are they doing a lot of nodding and agreeing, or are they offering observations and questions that are relevant to the conversation? As a quick test, throw out a question like "What do you think?" If they hesitate and 'um' a lot before replying, chances are, they are not fully engaged.

Use these three measurements to assess whether they are interested or ready to leave.

- Where are the person's eyes looking? At you? Or at everything else?
- Which way does their torso face? If it's away from you, they probably aren't interested.
- Is the person active in the conversation or are they simply agreeing? Throw a test question their way.

3. Master Micro-Expression Identification

Once you have assessed their level of interest, it is time to move on to more specific expressions. Obvious expressions like happiness will be easy to read. Smiling or laughing are fairly universal. However, most of the time people will try to hide their true feelings. This means you'll have to watch closely for minute clues. Pay attention to the face region, and listen to the tone of their voice.

Now ask a leading question. Despite the verbal answer, you'll see a flash of their true feeling if you look and listen closely. You'll have to study yourself and the people around you to get good at identifying micro-expressions, through online simulations can provide some extra practice. With experience, you'll be able to discern anger from disgust, fear from sadness, and happiness from surprise.

- Pay attention to a person's face during an interaction
- Pay attention to vocal tone and pauses
- Ask a leading, perhaps difficult question and see if the answer matches the facial response
- Practice by watching videos online of micro-expression tests

A couple of well-regarded sites for quick examples of this are:

- http://www.microexpressionstest.com/
- https://mazuzu.com/microexpressions/

Note: I am not affiliated with any of these websites and I can't guarantee they will remain live, but similar practice sites exist in a number of locations online. Search around to find some that work for you and have fun seeing if you can guess correctly.

4. Connect Cues and Results

The great thing about reading people and finding connections between visual cues and their behavior or results is that we do it already. We simply don't usually pay attention to it.

Take your reading one step further by starting to establish a few patterns you can rely on. The patterns you discover will be based on experience. The more closely you watch people, and yourself, the more you'll see these types of things start to appear. For example, have you ever watched a movie where there is a dramatic scene in a doctor's office? The doctor is vague on the details but firmly suggests more tests. You can't see into the doctor's mind, or their charts, and yet you can perceive that the results won't be good. In a later scene, your suspicions are confirmed.

How did you know? Because you recognized the tone and expressions from previous observations. This happens all the time in real life too. The more patterns you can perceive and put together, the better you'll be able to predict someone's behavior.

- Visit a coffee shop or public location and take a look at the people around you.
- Pick one and really notice how he/she moves and what they say through body language and verbal cues. Do they appear kind? Angry? Tense?
- Then look at what they do over the next few minutes. Did the cue match the result? It should.

5. Guess What Happens Next

So far, we've discussed several cues you can use to gather information. You have the tools you need to read someone fairly well, but will you get it right? You will sometimes, and other times you won't. After all, human's aren't robots. But still, we can improve our accuracy.

In order to become more accurate, you have to practice assessing a person's body language, facial expressions, tone, and so forth and then consciously make predictions about what they will physically do next. This can be a powerful skill to have in sports, combat arts or even just out on the street.

Take people's cues, and start to make a guess on what kind of person they are and how they will behave. Don't just take a quick glance and make assumptions. Make a conscious effort to look at all the aspects we already explored. Posture, body language, facial muscles, vocal tone, and speech. Are they leaning forward? If so, they are probably into the conversation. Are they leaning back, glancing around? In this case, they are probably not.

Many of these cues are already read-able, we just need to switch on the parts of our brain to recognize them at a conscious level.

- Once more, in a public environment, visit a local bar or restaurant and try to read people.
- Try to guess how they know one another,
- Guess how their interactions will turn out,
- Or even guess what they will order based on the questions they ask and their subtle responses. The more you practice, the better you will get at predicting patterns and guessing what will happen next.
- You can also practice at home. Use movies and TV to predict a character's actions based on how they move and speak.

6. Putting It All Together

If you have been following the steps, then you now have a very quick and effective method for reading anyone, but of course, results can vary. People are infinitely different and as such, so are their cues and responses. One thing I can guarantee, however, is that by practicing, you will get better.

Experiment with reading people in order to improve your success at work and in your personal life. If you can read people, then you can anticipate their needs and offer solutions. You'll also be able to notice communication patterns that are almost always successful—and make them your own.

Although this is the final step, you'll find that your skill is constantly evolving. The more time you spend reading people, the less they'll surprise you, that is true, but you'll always continue to pick up new patterns.

1. Become aware of your own cues by using a mirror and/or friends and family
2. Figure out if a person is engaged with a conversation by looking at the position or their chest and responses
3. Look at their face for micro-expressions and maybe practice spotting them yourself
4. Connect their cues to their actions and see if it matches up. Then think about why?
5. Start to make predictions from cues. Guess what a person will do next and see how accurate you are. Test it in public places.
6. Practice!

Applying What You Learned

Eventually, you'll be able to read people cold. However, don't expect to do it from day one. Instead, start with the first step—becoming more self-aware. Then work through the remaining five steps as your skill progresses. If you can identify what cues trigger certain emotions in yourself, then you will learn how to trigger the same response from others. One of the easiest ways to foster this essential foundation of self-awareness is to pay attention to the emotions you experience throughout the next few days. You might even write them down until you are able to connect each response with an external trigger. Remember, the better you can read yourself, the better you'll be able to read others.

Overall, these skills can be very powerful but even if you don't become a master mind-reader, you can have a lot of fun by simply sitting with a friend somewhere public and playing a game of guessing the story of the people around you and what they will do next, based on their body language, facial movement, and voice. Give it a go!

HOW TO SPOT A LIAR (THE 3-STEP SECRET CODE OF DECEPTION)

While most of this book is about the internal actions you can take to better yourself, or the techniques for improving your own mental abilities, I wanted to also show you a few powerful techniques for understanding the way others think, and indeed operate. One of these techniques and one that I have found invaluable in life is the ability to spot a liar.

You may believe yourself fairly adept at spotting deception in your daily life, but the truth is that we as a species are generally speaking quite awful at spotting when others are lying to us. Human nature makes us trusting and compliant. We want to believe others would never mean us harm and we like to think that they hold the same beliefs we do. Unfortunately , this just isn't the case and it's estimated that we may be lied to, on a small scale or large, up to two hundred times a day!

I know what you are thinking, and no, it's not all politicians either.

Deception in advertising, fibs from work colleagues, even white lies from family members crop up so often that our brains struggle to recognize all but the most obvious cases. Luckily there are a number of techniques you can use to increase your awareness and bring down that number.

The techniques below are not just proven, they are some of the top methods employed by global intelligence agencies around the world, such as the CIA, MI6, and Mossad to detect deception during interrogation. These agencies employ some of the best interrogators from around the world, and despite what you may think based on movies and TV, physical persuasion through torture or injury is far less likely to produce the results they need. Instead, they apply careful and meticulous layers of questioning, designed to reveal the truth behind a suspect's words.

For a further understanding of this subject, take a look at my chapter on how to read anyone.

As with any method regarding understanding another person's intentions, there is good and bad news:

The bad news: People are infinitely varied and weird. Body language, mannerisms, and overall composure vary not only between men and women but by age, location, culture and many more. Bottom line is that we can never be one-hundred percent sure when someone is lying. It's simply impossible and even governments, have to acknowledge that when they track down vital intelligence, there is always a margin for error. Simply put, people are unpredictable and no lie detection method works every time for every person.

The good news: Most people (80/90%) follow the same kinds of patterns and techniques when they employ deception. This means that with a little knowledge, some quick looking and awareness of what to look for, you can be fairly confident about the person you are speaking to and their intentions.

Let's take a look at the tips:

. . .

(First) Establish a baseline

Before you even begin analyzing the person in question, you need to establish a baseline. By this, I mean that you need to know what your target looks like and how they act while telling the truth before you can start to spot deception.

Sure, if they are a friend or family member, you are probably already quite familiar with how they move and present themselves, but are you familiar with how they act under pressure? Perhaps not.

Also, what happens if the person you need to question is a stranger or an unfamiliar work colleague? In this case, we have no idea if acting like a fidgety addict is part of their normal behavior or a signal of big fat lies. So, before you start getting into interrogation mode, keep things casual and relaxed, to prevent the target clamming up early. In fact, I wouldn't even suggest approaching the main subject initially.

- The first thing to do is establish a relaxed environment, where the target doesn't immediately feel threatened. If they do feel threatened, it will be hard to read deception amid the ambient anxiety.
- Next, ask them two or three low-stress questions that they should easily answer. EG, "Do you know if we have enough milk in the fridge?" or "Have you seen John lately?"
- Closely observe their body language and behavior. Do they cross their arms? Look around? What about posture? Tense or relaxed?
- This is your baseline. Now, when looking for signs of a lie, each signal should be outside the normal behavior patterns you just witnessed.

1. Blocking (Physical and verbal)

Perhaps one of the most obvious methods for detecting deception is looking for 'blocking'; that is the subject either physically or verbally trying to put things between the two of you, as a method of hiding their falsehoods.

When we lie we feel threatened by the opposition, in this case, the person we are lying to. This leads us to subconsciously want to defend ourselves, both by our body language and our verbal cues. Imagine if a person threatened you on the street with violence, how would you react? Raise your hands to protect yourself? Get angry? Get defensive?

All of these are great cues that a person is also lying.

Physically, the signs of deception are more obvious than verbal. Essentially, we are looking for any action which creates a barrier between the words coming out of their mouth and you. The most common presentations include

1. Folding arms

Folded arms are the most common subconscious reaction. The liar is creating a physical block between the two of you

2. Hands blocking the face and mouth

If the liar is constantly touching their mouth, blocking parts of their face or touching around the nose, this can be a strong signal of deception, as they are trying to filter the words through their hands, before they reach you.

3. Crossed arms or legs

Similar to the folded arms position, this action is often more visible if your opposition is seated. When we feel threatened, we pulled our limbs in tight and feel like keeping to ourself.

4. Becoming smaller

No, this doesn't mean curling up in a ball on the floor – although some children may adopt this, but when we are relaxed and open with someone, we feel comfortable enough to spread our limbs wide, perhaps place our palms wide on the table or sit in a relaxed posture. Under threat or deception – the opposite is true

5. Putting objects in the way

This one can be a little harder to spot, depending on the environment in

question, but simply put when someone is lying, they will often position themselves on the opposite side of a large object, such as a table, chair or some other
furniture as a way to create the block, without having to do it themselves.

So do these guarantee a liar? Alone, no. But they are a great starting point to
observe when looking for signs of a lie. Let's look at the second cue.

2. Redirection

The bottom line is that people don't like confrontation and especially don't
like lying to someone's face. When you confront someone directly and ask
them up front "Hey, did you take this?" They will often employ 'redirection' in
a subconscious effort to take some of the heat off themselves.

Redirection is a little more subtle than blocking but still offers a strong
indication of deception in a person trying to cover something up. In this case,
the verbal response from an individual after you have questioned them should
be carefully observed as much as the physical.

Often their response will be to move the conversation onto something else
altogether or to only partially answer your query by steering the subject elsewhere. It can be a little difficult to spot, however, and if you aren't careful, you
may find yourself quickly talking about something else altogether and the liar,
getting away with it.

Here's an example:

Let's say some money goes missing from your shared apartment. You
suspect a friend, but want to find out.

You go directly to the friend and ask "Did you take the money from my room?"

They respond. "How can you ask that? What kind of person do you take
me for?"

. . .

See what happened here? While their response may seem emotional and heartfelt, they haven't actually answered the question at all. They have redirected the question completely. Typically this kind of response would then be followed by some kind of blocking. (They get out their phone and start fiddling with it, or they move behind a table or to the other side of the room.)

So does redirecting immediately make them guilty? No, but many liars will try to weave as much truth and misdirection into their responses as possible in a way to make them feel better about their responses.

If you look at the above example, the friend in question hasn't even lied yet. They have deceived, sure. But not lied.

Another addition to this is adding qualifiers to their story, as a way of diffusing the lie.

Asked again. "Did you take the money from my room?"

They answer. "I would never take money from your wallet on the side."

Here they are not only redirecting, but adding additional details. Maybe the money was taken from a drawer or table, but they are throwing in the wallet idea as a way to diffuse the lie. The more pressure that comes from your questioning, the more elaborate the lie may become, to the point where a complex and meandering story has evolved from your original question.

Again, these cues alone do not guarantee a liar but combined with the physical act of blocking, you should now start to develop an idea of how to spot the signs of deception.

Let's take a look at the final test.

3. The Timeline

When someone lies convincingly and is not showing any significant body language to indicate deception, and they don't redirect or add extraneous information, there is one final test you can apply and that is to check their timeline.

When we take part in deception, it's relatively easy to concoct falsehoods about specific parts of an event. That is to say, it's not too difficult to mentally come up with a simple lie about, not taking money, not speaking to an ex or to implicate someone else in something. However, the one thing that is much harder is to fabricate an entire timeline based on those events.

As such, pushing someone on the exact order things happened can often, throw off their mental processing and reveal a lie. This is especially true if you ask them to recreate the series of events out of order. IE Not sequential.

This non-sequential trick makes lying even harder because the liar now not only has to fabricate the event itself but all the surrounding events leading up to it. While they may be able to manage this, the focus required to generate such a thing makes it much harder for them to be self-aware and as such, you will likely now start to see evidence of blocking or redirection.

Liars, whether they are making things up there and then or they have rehearsed a well thought out deception, have often done it before but they almost always lie in a chronological fashion. This means that in their head, they have decided the sequence of events starting at the beginning and finishing at the end- because that's how human beings work. It makes sense to them. But if you suddenly pull details of the lie out of the normal time sequence you can often trip them up on the details.

Going back to the stolen money angle you may approach your friend in the following way.

"So how did the money end up missing at the end of the day?" (The end of the sequence)

"What time did you get home?" (The start of the sequence)

"When did you walk into the room?" (The midpoint)

If something has happened and you suspect deception, you can confront the *possible* liar by throwing questions about the series of events at them out of the normal order. Don't give them too much time to think about it, before moving onto the next inquiry. All the while, keep an eye out for the other cues, like blocking and redirection.

Checking the timeline example:

1. Start with a question about the final part of the deception
2. Throw in an inquiry about the start
3. Finish by querying the middle of the events
4. Finally, check if everything matches up? Observes their behavior for other cues.

Summary

So let's briefly recap the techniques when confronting someone you suspect of lying.

1. Blocking. Look for physical movements the person in question is making to put barriers between you two. Could be furniture, distance or even hands and arms.
2. Redirection. Look for them steering the conversation in irrelevant directions or adding extraneous information to distract from the lie.
3. Check the Timeline. Quiz them on the events out of chronological order. See if the story still stacks up.

So, are they telling the truth?

If the individual passes all the above tests, does that mean they are telling the truth? Not necessarily, but it is more likely. It's incredibly hard for us to maintain control of our physical, mental and verbal actions under pressure and unless the person you are quizzing has years of practice, it's unlikely they will manage to clear all of these tests without showing a few tells.

So, if they show some of the signs above, are they definitely lying? Again, it's likely but not necessarily about what you think. Remember, that these tests are to detect deception not specific lies and can reveal more than you realize.

For example, let's say you question a co-worker about using the last of the coffee in the office. They claim it wasn't them and you diligently press ahead with checking for some of the 'tells' from above while asking if they know what happened to the coffee. Your co-worker is displaying deception signals – so they are guilty, right?

Maybe. Or maybe someone else used the last of the coffee and your co-worker knows who it is but doesn't want to be the office snitch. They would still display deception, as the stress of the knowledge gets to them, but they are technically not guilty.

As such, specific questions are important when establishing events and indeed deception.

EXERCISE: LEARN TO SPOT A LIE IN 3 MINUTES

This is a fun little exercise you can play with friends or family members, which has the additional benefit of teaching you the basics of lie detection and offering a chance to test observing the cues you have learned above.

While the game can be challenging under normal circumstances, it also makes a great drinking game between friends. Alcohol tends to reduce inhibitions and means that liars are far more likely to demonstrate the 'tells' we talked about earlier when they can't fully control their responses.

It's also why, during the cold war, American and Soviet agents, would often approach rival operatives at a bar or pub, and attempt to extract intelligence while getting them drunk.

One or two beers, or similar low-strength drinks, tend to be best. Any less and they are near stone-cold sober and in control. Any more and they tend to be tipping over toward drunk, and any responses prove unreliable.

Just make sure you don't drink too much yourself, or you will lose any advantage offered by the alcoholic lubrication of your friends!

The game is called Two Truths, One Lie, and it's quite simple.

1. You must tell your friend three things they don't already know about you
2. Two of these things must be true
3. One must be a lie

4. They get to ask you one question about any of the statements
5. They must guess the lie, with only one attempt

Now comes the fun part. Swap over and get them to do the same. They must tell you two truths and one lie. You can ask one question about any of the statements. You, with the knowledge of spotting a liar, should find it easier.

1. First, look for physical discomfort and in particular **blocking**
2. Look for **redirection.** Is one of their statements vague and meandering? Do they redirect your question to something else?
3. Think about the **timeline.** Do any of the statements not add up in terms of date and time? Push them on the exact order of events.

To make the game more fun, or more challenging depending on how you view it, another option is to add one question after the statements. IE after your friend has given you the three statements, you are allowed one question to query any of them or all of them. Be direct and push them on the one you suspect the most. Look for the cues.

TRAIN YOUR BRAIN TO HANDLE ADRENALINE

The ability to handle stress and the acute form of stress–panic–is an incredible skill to have, one that can literally be life and death in the case of a dangerous situation like a violent encounter or a sudden medical emergency. It's also a skill that few possess because training for true panic is surprisingly difficult.

The following technique is a simple training method employed by some self-defense schools to teach their students the feeling of panic and to allow the body to become accustomed to the sensation.

The Truth about Panic and Training for Adrenaline

Adrenaline is a wonderful thing. It enables us to be alert and focused, it instantly wakes up the body in an unexpected situation and it can stimulate muscles beyond their normal capacity. Heck, adrenaline can even save lives when injected for allergic anaphylaxis. (As a peanut allergy sufferer this one is particularly appealing)

But Adrenaline also has a darker side. It throws your body into overdrive, pushing every system beyond its normal limits causing confusion, irrational behavior, and a massive comedown after the event.

In self-defense or sudden stress terms Adrenaline gives us clarity and focus in a violent encounter and enables us to fight harder, run faster or last longer than usual...but at a cost.

Adrenaline also triggers panic. Panic is the dangerous byproduct of the hyper-mode our body goes through in a threat situation.

Panic clouds our judgment distorts our decisions and can make us act on pure emotion. This can be especially dangerous when we are angry or around the vengeful, feelings that could easily occur after a sudden violent incident.

Training for panic

If you could train your mind to deal with panic it would be a big help, right?

Quite simply it is very hard to fool the body into reacting like it would in a real life-or-death situation. Somewhere, no matter how deep, our brain always knows when it is training. I.e. not really under threat. The way to get around this is to take away the one thing it always needs – air.

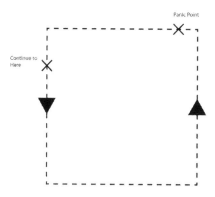

IMPORTANT: Don't attempt the following exercise if you have any medical conditions or without supervision. This is just an explanation of a technique that worked for many self-defense students; try it at your own risk. Oh and don't push yourself too far, it doesn't help!

To induce panic in a controlled way try the following:

- Within a gym or large area work out a route around the outside.
- Start by walking around this route at a normal pace.

- After one lap, now hold your breath.
- Keep walking as before at the same pace
- Eventually you will start to feel desperate to breathe (Panic sets in)
- Get to the point when you <u>really</u> need to take a breath
- Take 5 more steps and raise an arm during these steps to signal the panic.
- After the 5 steps breathe normally and relax.

During this last part, your body is experiencing panic, or as close to the real thing as you can get. The desperate need for air triggers the adrenaline and all the associated reactions with it.

If you can learn to control this sensation, relax your body and mind, you can eventually control the panic reaction.

The exercise can be ramped up by jogging or even practicing hitting a focus pad for a short period while holding your breath.

Top Tip: Don't do it until you pass out! This can cause long term damage!

HOW TO DEAL WITH PANIC

While all of us suffer from nerves at some point, when things get really out of control we can suffer from a panic attack and this can be debilitating for performance.

A panic attack is a much more acute (short-term) form of tension that affects the body in powerful and usually negative ways. It can seem like a terrible, life-threatening experience when it hits, though it's not fatal at all.

A panic attack can manifest in many different ways depending on the individual. It usually includes rapid breathing, increased heart rate, and a sense of danger or dread. This can be particularly traumatic the first time you experience it. Panic attacks may commonly occur right before a stressful event like a competition or performance of some sort.

The truth is that while panic may feel awful it is an evolutionary response to a dangerous situation. In our prehistoric days, a sudden threat like a hungry saber-toothed tiger showing up would rightly inspire a rapid heart rate to prepare the body for fight or flight. This rush of adrenaline enabled us to run faster, work harder, and fight for our lives if the situation required it.

Today the danger is less likely to be a marauding carnivore, but the response is still coded into our DNA. Hence when something quickly and powerfully stresses us out, it can trigger this overwhelming sensation.

The first reassuring fact to realize is that no one has ever died from a panic attack. It may not feel nice, and you may even think you are running out of breath. However, the body is amazingly resilient and adaptable. You may feel like you're dying, but you're not. Panic attacks have never (directly) caused a fatality. If you're driving when you have a panic attack, pull off the road until it passes. Just keep yourself safe. Call 911 (for the US) or your country's emergency number if you need to. They'll help you if it's just a panic attack. Just because it's not fatal doesn't mean panic isn't debilitating. In a difficult situation, we need to be clear-headed and able to respond quickly. So how do we manage the sudden onset of panic that arises from nerves?

Understanding the Process

The trick to beating a panic attack lies in understanding what is happening in your brain when one hits — really understanding. The more you know, the more you can pull yourself out of a panic attack.

As we've already discussed, a panic attack is a primal response to a threat. You may not know that it also turns your brain primal. When a huge dump of adrenaline or stress hormones like cortisol hits our body, the brain starts to shut down higher reasoning sections in favor of the more instinctive parts.

It's a little like hypothermia. When your body gets cold enough, it cuts off the blood supply to the limbs to save your body. The brain does roughly the same thing. During panic, it reduces blood flow and activity in the outer (higher reasoning and intelligence) areas of the brain. Then it sends all the blood to the core sections like the Amygdala – the region responsible for fight or flight.

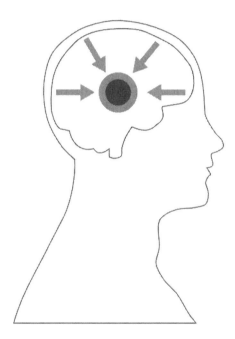

This reaction means that, yes, we are temporarily energized for action but at the cost of rational thought. A sensation that may have been common tens of thousands of years ago overwhelms us today.

. . .

The Solution

The way to counter this reaction is quite simple. We want to activate the whole brain (and body) again and increase blood flow to the higher functioning areas. This then re-starts our intelligent reasoning, taking control of and reducing the sensation of panic. There are, in fact, lots of recommended methods used by psychologists to achieve this. Here are two simple ones which approach the problem from different angles.

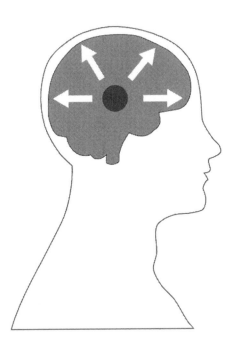

The Countdown Technique

When panic or acute nerves hit, start at 200 and mentally count down in sevens, focusing on how far you get. This approach engages the mathematical part of the brain and forces it to re-engage the higher levels of reasoning, reducing the panic reaction.

We count down in sevens because this has been shown to be one of the hardest numbers to reduce each time – thereby requiring actual thought. If you used fives or tens, there is a chance it would not engage enough of your mind.

Just begin at 200 and slowly reduce the number, taking time to subtract 7 on each count. 200…193…186…etc.

Get Moving

When panic hits, go for a walk or a light jog, depending on your fitness level.

We know that during a panic there is too much activity in our inner brain. So, put the body in motion. This increases the blood flow to the extremities and reduces the stress reaction.

You don't need to kill yourself sprinting to use this method. Simply engaging the whole body is enough in most cases. Walk, jog or shake your limbs off to improve circulation.

Beat Panic by Not Escaping It

In managing panic, it's essential to "beat" whatever it is that triggers your stress, not escape it, despite how uncomfortable it may seem at the time.

If for example, you hate crowds and start to panic in one but then go somewhere quiet until you feel better, you are, in fact, positively reinforcing the notion that you feel better when you escape. The more times you do this, the stronger the idea becomes in your mind until you eventually realize you can no longer go anywhere with a crowd. A pattern has formed.

Instead, a better approach is to learn "Exposure Therapy." This technique physically and mentally introduces you to the stress trigger or phobia and allows you to process how non-threatening it really is. It has been established as an effective treatment for everything from PTSD (Post Traumatic Stress Disorder) to OCD (Obsessive Compulsive Disorder), both of which are very stressful conditions.

It is closely connected to a principle famously known as "Pavlovian Extinction." This technique uses repeated exposure to a "trigger" or threat that doesn't cause the negative result expected. This eventually results in the brain no longer associating the trigger with the negative result, thereby breaking the pattern.

How do I do it?

Jokes about "exposing yourself" aside, the process for removing stress triggers through Exposure Therapy is actually rather straight forward. It involves the gradual and measured introduction of the stressor and positive re-enforcement of the exposure. It is sometimes also known as systematic desensitization. The technique works best when aided by a therapist or even a friend.

The principle is to first assess the hierarchy of the stimulus or the potential triggers causing panic and establish a series of stressors from least-stressful/panic-inducing to most stressful/panic-inducing. Then you simply start with the least-stressful experience and, using methods of controlled breathing or types of meditation (as discussed elsewhere in this book), you gradually spend time in the presence of the panic trigger. Once the easiest one has been conquered, move on to the next and so on until the final and most stressful situation has been desensitized.

To see how it works, let's go back to the panic induced by crowds (Agoraphobia). Imagine that you suffer great stress from the concept of being in a huge crowd at a sports event.

Your stress triggers, ranging from easiest to worst, might be:

- A picture of a crowd
- Seeing a small crowd from a distance
- Seeing a large crowd not far away
- Being part of a small crowd
- Being part of a large crowd (at the event)

Starting with the picture of a crowd you would allow yourself to fully engage with the image and experience the stress. Then, use controlled breathing or your choice of technique to reduce the stress levels. Do this while maintaining close proximity to the picture. Once you have mastered this several times, you can move onto the next level of stress and repeat the same procedure.

The goal, of course, is to ultimately desensitize yourself to the final and most panic-inducing level. If you find you cannot cope at any given level, that's fine. Do your best to stay at that tier, but if you must remove it simply drop back to the previous one. Don't abandon the process altogether.

This process is widely recommended by health professionals and psychologists worldwide. It has proven successful in dealing with everything from panic to phobias and anxiety. The brief description above gives a helpful overview. It is recommended that you read more on 'Exposure Therapy' and 'Systematic Desensitization' if you are interested in using this approach.

This is quite an involved technique and its usefulness depends on how much the stress trigger affects your daily life. If for example, you are terrified of snakes but live in a country without any, it's unlikely to affect your daily activity. You don't need to force yourself to the nearest zoo to handle some venomous reptiles. (Although overcoming something like this can be rewarding for anyone!)

On the other hand, if you get panicked near water, it would definitely be worthwhile to become exposed to the sensation of water. You can learn how much fun water can be.

THE MOST POWERFUL TECHNIQUE FOR OVERALL MENTAL STRENGTH

There are many methods included within this book for making the most of your mind's potential but one technique stands head and shoulders above the rest and could be said to be the foundation behind 80% of the others.

In fact, if you take nothing else away from this book, then this one tactic will still help you make massive improvements in sports, in competition and in life.

Mindfulness

Mindfulness is a principle often associated with meditation. It can have excellent benefits when combined with forms of meditation, but it doesn't have to involve any Lotus positions or hours of personal reflection.

Indeed, mindfulness is scientifically proven to be so effective that health organizations around the world, such as the UK's NHS recommend it as a method for combatting depression, Obsessive Compulsive Disorder, and many other mental conditions.

Practicing mindfulness not only helps treat negative mental issues but also builds and strengthens positive awareness of the moment you are in.

So what is Mindfulness?

Mindfulness is, in essence, simply about being in the moment and observing your experience of that moment without judgment. It is a skill that is both easy to start and difficult to master. Luckily, even the act of attempting it yields great benefits. Once it is practiced on a regular basis, your brain starts to develop strong, positive behaviors.

We spend so much of our lives planning, plotting and working out where and who we want to be. It's only natural, after all, to have dreams and desires. But continually focusing on the future is an extremely fast way to get stressed.

The future isn't here. We can't directly affect it right now so why spend all of our time thinking about it?

The same is true of the past. How many times have you regretted something, caught yourself remembering former loves or times you wish you could have changed?

So much of our time is spent looking forward and back at the infinite possibilities of what might be that we hardly ever focus on what is.

A core concept of almost every form of meditation is to switch off these thoughts of past and future and just be.

Don't worry about what was or what could be. There is just the here and now. Fully focus on the sensations and feelings of the moment you are in and only that moment.

Anytime you feel stressed or wish to calm your thoughts, begin by thinking *"how do I feel right now?"* This is the central principle behind many of the techniques described in this guide.

Exercise: How to get Started with Mindfulness

Mindfulness is always a personal experience and so what works for one person may not always work for another. That said, there are steps you can take right now to begin developing the skill of mindfulness in your own way.

1. **Location.** Find a quiet area where you can have some privacy. It can be within your home, office, garden, place of worship, or outside. Mindfulness can be practiced anywhere, even at busy, stressful events and competitions. But to start with, try to find a place where you are able to relax that is free of distractions.

2. **Position.** Make yourself comfortable. Try to remain seated either

on the floor or in a chair because lying down may cause you to fall asleep. Straighten your spine.

3. **Focus.** Choose a focal point. This can be internal or external. Focus on a feeling, an image in your mind, an object, a candle's flame, a word or a phrase. You may choose to keep your eyes opened or closed depending on what is most comfortable. As an easy starting point try to focus on your breath for a count of four, in and out.

4. **No judgment.** Try to maintain an observant, yet nonjudgmental, mindset. This is crucial. Allow your thoughts to move through your mind as you shift back to your focal point. Try not to waste energy worrying about whether you are doing this right. Remember, the goal is relaxation. Keep breathing.

5. **Be in the moment.** Any time your mind drifts, simply bring your thoughts back to the moment you are in. Focus on your breath, how your body feels, or your focal point. Try to bring your thoughts away from worrying about things to come or things you have to do.

6. **Short and regular.** Maintain this for around 2 minutes. As it becomes easier, you can try to increase the duration or practice the skills in more stressful environments but start small. After you finish, slow down and try to maintain the calm in your day.

II

PART TWO: ANALYZE AND RESPOND

Once the body and mind are calm, collected and panic-free it is time to assess the situation using all of your skills and choose how to react. Intelligent understanding of different personality types and how you should treat them can go a long way to asserting dominance in a tricky situation – be that a violent encounter on the street or a difficult office meeting!

Note that our aim in the next section is to respond, rather than react. We are intelligently choosing our actions and deliberately using our brains.

The following techniques show how you can discover the hidden side of any opponent and how you can respond by generating instant cool and calm even in the tensest situation.

STAND UP FOR YOURSELF (THE SMART WAY)

Defending Your Message Without Being Aggressive

We are all made up of beliefs and some of those core ideals are so strong that they become part of who we are. They are our foundation. Immovable. As such, it can be important when others disagree with your core values to get your point across and convey your ideals in a confident assertive manner.

Your message may be powerful, but unfortunately, that doesn't mean everyone will agree with it. So how can you get people to respect your position, your ideas and listen to what you have to say?

We take a huge risk by assuming we can force people to hear us out, respect our space or believe what we believe. Ideals just don't work that way and you can't gain respect by being a bully. The more aggressive you are, the more resistant your audience will become. The first part of this discussion will reveal four positive strategies for making people more willing to listen to your message.

These involve understanding, improving communication and really trying to connect to another person, using some simple tactics which will make them much more likely to see your side of the story.

However, I don't want to mislead you into thinking these strategies will work every time. Unfortunately, life is not that easy. When sharing controversial opinions, ideas or even just personal thoughts even in the most peaceful manner, you still may encounter people who will respond with serious judgment or passive aggression. That's why the second part of this chapter will focus on my five-step plan for dealing with aggressive behavior without dropping down to their level. These techniques are excellent for keeping your cool, asserting your dominance over the situation and most importantly, allowing you to avoid risking life or limb.

You'll find that you can apply both of these strategies to many different scenarios in your life.

PART 1: HOW TO GET RESPECT FROM YOUR OPPONENT, FAST

Getting A Good Response

The first steps to taking control of conflict and an increasing opposition is to establish respect. If an opponent respects you, it's incredibly hard for them to dislike you, and as such, they become much more receptive to your presence, way of thinking and ideas. In a physical confrontation, this method makes it near impossible for an opponent to see you as a target.

To truly get your message across, you must build this bond of mutual respect fast, in much the same way that rival boxers, football teams or athletes, might be fierce competitors, but have a lot of respect for the each other's abilities come competition time.

The following tips offer quick techniques for building that early connection.

1. Validate The Other Side – Find common ground.

You'll have no trouble connecting with people who already agree. It is people who don't share your beliefs who you will need to convince. The key to being able to do this without alienating them is to offer some validation for at least part of their view. Tell them that you can understand their reasoning because of certain evidence.

For example, let's say you are a Jets fan but you meet a Giants supporter. You might disagree on almost everything, but by at least acknowledging a single good play or an outstanding performance in one game from the rival team, you suddenly make them more interested in what you have to say.

In a competitive environment, it could even be as simple as joking about how bad the weather is with a rival.

This commonality will make them more willing to listen. When someone disagrees with you, or judges you, it becomes impossible to then change sides and agree, no matter how much sense they make. So, don't back your audience into a corner. Validate *parts* of their stance with small examples, then give them an alternate view to think about. One of the best ways to do this is by posing a hypothetical question which you can then answer with concrete information.

- Find at least one (small) thing you can agree on and use that to build a connection
- When you have mutual respect, press your position, but don't attack them personally
- Try to see things from their point of view, even if you don't agree with it
- Use hypotheticals and evidence to support any viewpoints you have

2. Let Them Save Face

In Asia and other parts of the middle east, the concept of saving face or keeping is a huge cultural idea. The concept is one of quite simply not looking like an idiot in a social environment and avoiding embarrassment at all costs. In the west, this is still valid, but we are far more comfortable with screaming matches on the street (even if perhaps we shouldn't be) but people still don't like to be humiliated.

When you have built a connection through the previous technique and you have an active listener who is willing to engage in your thinking, be sure to proceed respectfully. Let them know that while you may disagree, you can still respect their beliefs and that you are in no way attacking them or their intelligence. Never make anyone feel dumb in any way. You don't want to insult or alienate anyone. Instead, make a genuine effort to understand their beliefs. When you do manage to sway their opinion, allow them to save face.

- Respect flows both ways. Demonstrate it.
- Disagree on ideas or viewpoints, but avoid antagonizing someone by keeping the discussion on-topic
- In other words, never attack them or their personality
- Don't humiliate, show empathy
- Acknowledge their viewpoint, and if they change it, don't gloat

3. Keep Their Attention Engaged

Even if your listener starts out interested, they'll lose focus if all you offer is dry facts. Instead, offer interesting stories, historical context, and various perspectives. Don't just pick one either, use a number of examples. The one caveat is that you don't want to just throw out random ideas, make sure all your examples tie together cohesively and clearly. Animate your conversation to keep your listener engaged, and keep asking their opinion until the very end.

- Throwing pure facts and figures at someone rarely works
- Apply stats or evidence to a personal opinion or experience to keep it engaging
- Use your hands and body language to keep their eyes moving
- Get their input, but don't let them control the discussion

4. Add A Sense Of Truth With Familiar Examples

The final strategy for getting people to respect your position, listen to you and agree with your message is to use examples with which they are already familiar. These are sometimes termed archetypes. The most familiar archetypes are found in fairytales and fables, used to convey a moral lesson. These ideas resonate with people of all ages and from all different backgrounds and are foundational blocks to good character.

Let's say you are calling someone out on being deceptive. You might use the example of the boy who cried wolf. It's a widely known story with a strong moral about the dangers of lying. Of course, the key is to only mention it and not become preachy.

Use examples that your audience will intuitively understand and connect with deeply. Because these values are accepted as true, connecting your point with them will also make your message seem inherently true. If you can connect with people in this way, then you can change their minds.

- Attach your ideas to familiar truths. Something undeniable.
- If you have a chance ahead of time, think of a famous story or fable supporting your point
- Consider the deeper meaning behind your point, and how the other person might connect to it.

PART 2: HOW TO DEFEND YOURSELF IN A RISING CONFLICT

Dealing With A Negative Response – Standing up for yourself the right way.

Let's assume things aren't quite going to plan and despite your best efforts to engage the other person with the previous techniques, things are becoming a bit hostile. It's time to stand up for yourself, but to do so in a confident and non-aggressive manner which will demonstrate assertiveness and control, often pushing your opposition to back down.

Understand that the point of the following techniques is absolutely not to escalate the situation. In fact, it's the opposite. The idea is to prevent a shouting match, to prevent a full-on confrontation and any violence.

1. Establish Eye Contact

Not everyone will allow a real connection. Sometimes because they are busy or focused elsewhere, but there are also people who will resist a connection because they disagree so much that they feel aggressive towards you. I say "feel aggressive" because they often don't have the guts to lash out physically or say something directly. Instead, they will let their true colors show passively.

If you have any practice reading people, then you'll be able to tell when they are about to get ugly. Often, the only thing you need to do to get them to rethink their approach is to look them directly in the eyes and maintain steady contact. There is no need to give them laser vision or act like a crazed hypnotist. Simply keep your eyes relaxed, but with attention fixed on the opponent.

This tells them that you know what they are doing and you aren't going to be intimidated.

- Fix your opponent with a relaxed but consistent gaze.
- Don't frown or try to stare them out just keep looking.
- Try to keep your hands away from your face.
- Practice on yourself (it can be surprisingly tricky). Try one minute in the mirror beforehand.

2. Let it Slide - Once

Note that in establishing eye contact you haven't done anything obvious or aggressive, yet you've sent a clear message that you aren't backing down. But what if your instincts were off? Try not to jump to conclusions. It could be that you are reading the situation wrong and the other person didn't mean anything aggressive at all. Misunderstandings are common, so it is smart to give them the benefit of the doubt—once. Proceed calmly and answer any questions at face value while still maintaining that eye contact. Give your companion a chance to change their tone. Their response will tell you everything you need to know.

- In conversation or an encounter with someone new, assume the best but prepare for the worst.
- Engage a person at face value initially. Don't assume anything.
- Allow them the benefit of the doubt, but only once.
- Monitor their responses. Was their first suggestions of aggression actually just a mistake, or are they increasingly hostile or passive-aggressive?

3. Let Them Know You Are Onto Them

Up until this point, our encounter has been focused on passively assessing someone, and presenting ourselves in a certain way. Now though, after we've tried all the other techniques and still notice someone trying to actively attack us through either actions or words, we need to act.

Most opponents will read your tone and body language enough to back off. However, some will persist. So, what do you do when someone is trying to push you off the edge?

If they persist after you have given them the eye-contact, the benefit of the doubt, and the warning, then it is time to be more direct. Don't let their bad behavior continue. Tell them flat-out that you know where they are trying to lead you, but that's not where you are going. You may be able to diffuse the situation by asking what their purpose is. They will likely be nervous when they respond, but don't back down and stay clear. If your companion continues to maintain their passive aggression, then there is only one thing left to do.

Give them a clear but polite warning. Are they asking probing questions designed to lock you into saying something that goes against your character? Reframe the question to ensure the answer is congruent with the way you want to be perceived. Are they manipulating the situation or your behavior? Don't fall for it. Call them out and tell them that you are not going to be coerced or attacked. Don't get aggressive, but be direct. Bottom line, don't let their bad behavior stand.

- Maintain eye contact, straighten your posture and take a deep breath.
- Address the other persons attack directly and let them know you are aware of it. (Most manipulators struggle with direct confrontation.)
- Let them know clearly, that you will not play the game they have in mind.
- Ask why they are doing it?
- If you prefer not to get into a debate, simply shake your head and stop talking. This not only signals you are not falling for their nonsense but adds a certain mystery to your actions, sometimes making an opponent hesitate.

4. Know When To Leave

At this point, you are probably getting upset. Most people will begin to freak out a little, based on natural self-preservation instincts. No doubt you are feeling attacked and the adrenaline is beginning to surge. Your reaction is important here so unless you are in physical danger, do your best not to react at all.

Stay cool and calm, at least on the surface and keep the conversation civil. Remind your opponent that you told them you would not entertain such behavior, then get up and walk away. Don't run, shout, or make a scene, simply leave. There is absolutely no reason you should have to put up with passive aggressive attacks, character assassinations, manipulation or aggression of any form, so don't. Be a better person.

- Breathe. Stay calm.
- Call them out on their behavior one last time, and tell them you are done.
- Get up, walk away or just leave the room. Take a minute to calm yourself.
- If things start to escalate before you leave, use raised palms. This not only shows a peaceful, calming gesture but also gives you a guard if the worst happens and physical confrontation starts.

Applying What You Learned

I hope you find these quick tips helpful.

We've explored the importance of considering your audience while sharing engaging stories they can connect with. This is one of the best ways to gain respect and get people to listen without being in-your-face aggressive. Give your audience a chance to speak up, too. Let them know you value their contributions.

Keep practicing to become an active listener in every conversation. The more you listen to the other side, the better equipped you will be in presenting the right information to defend your message. Be prepared to meet resistance though. Study the five steps to dealing with passive and active aggression so you can react in a calm and respectful manner every time. Never let another bully pull you down to their level again.

Be a better person. Be the stronger person.

PERSONALITY TYPES AND HOW YOU CAN OVERCOME THEM

One of the most useful skills in life is being able to assess an opponent (or ally) and work out what kind of personality they have and the relative strengths and weaknesses of that personality type. Once you have this information you can then choose which route of approach to take when dealing with them.

In any direct physical competition, like sport, this can be a very powerful skill to have. This determination suggests which approach you should take when competing. Should you, for example, be aggressive and direct or gentle and circuitous, work straight toward the goal or play off their emotions?

Modern psychology categorizes people in one of six initial personality types, and although there are several schools of thought on this, these types are the most commonly used:

Extravert, Introvert, Sensing, Intuitive, Feeling or Thinking

How to spot them

Although people are all different and there are many shades in between each personality type there are some solid indicators of what kind of person you are dealing with and you can adjust your interaction with them accordingly.

. . .

Extravert vs Introvert

The difference between an Extravert and Introvert is mainly attitude. Does the person in question act first and then think about it (Extraverts), or do they consider all the options before acting? (Introverts).

Extraverts:

Strengths: Typically outgoing, social and personable. Liked by peers and bold in choices. Often popular.

Weaknesses: Doesn't always think things through. Can have poor attention to detail.

Introverts:

Strengths: Tactically minded, makes solid choices based on logic and information. Can often see the bigger picture.

Weaknesses: Lacks impulsiveness and spontaneity. Can be slow to react to change. Not always comfortable in front of others.

Sensing vs Intuitive

When we gather information in life we use our five senses. How we do this determines whether we sense or guess our way through things. Does the person trust all their senses and then analyze the data? (Sensing) or do they simply go on gut feeling most of the time? (Intuitive).

Sensing

Strengths: Analytical and observant. Often great at seeing patterns and trends. Strong predictive skills.

Weaknesses: Struggles to act on instinct. Can be slow to react in sudden situations.

Intuitive

Strengths: Strong moral compass. Great natural reading instincts for people and situations

Weaknesses: May ignore the facts. Can struggle with logic-based challenges.

. . .

Thinking vs Feeling

How does the person make decisions? Do they use logical, objective arguments (Thinking) or do they simply go with empathy or what feels right? (Feeling)

Thinking

Strengths: Good at establishing tactics based on facts and figures. Strong logic skills.

Weaknesses: May not understand how others feel. Can struggle to connect with people.

Feeling

Strengths: Very empathic. Can relate to others and offer guidance and support easily.

Weaknesses: May ignore facts and figures in favor of a feeling. Can be illogical.

Test Yourself

Of course, these are broad personality bandings and individuals may exhibit aspects of multiple types. However, we all demonstrate one type that is more dominant than the others so always look out for the most obvious sign of a person's type.

See if you can figure out which type of person you are dealing with in the following scenario and how you should approach them.

Scenario 1:

At work, a rival is standing around laughing and loudly telling everyone about a recent skydiving trip he made just because he 'felt like it'. People laugh along with him and seem entertained.

Answer:

This type of person exhibits classic extrovert behavior; acting on impulse and being socially engaged. You wouldn't overcome someone like this by being equally loud and spontaneous. Instead, focus on detail and strategy; something they will likely overlook.

Scenario 2:

At a sports tournament, you overhear a rival competitor talking to an injured teammate. They are sympathetic and offering words of help and support. They seem genuinely sad for their colleague.

Answer:

This type of person is showing largely 'Feeling' behavior, sharing sensations with their team.

This kind of individual can be easily overcome by making them choose between gut feeling and logic. By forcing a choice between attending the injured player and the outcome of the match you could create a discord with their personality type, giving you the edge.

High Machs

High Machiavellians or 'High Machs' are an interesting additional personality group that could, in theory, fall into any of the others.

Named after infamous renaissance philosopher Niccolò Machiavelli, these individuals see no problem with deceit and manipulation to get their way. It's not that they are *bad* people inherently, more that they have little care or concept for good and bad. In fact, in some cases, this is a great strength. For them, the ends always justify the means.

Spotting High Machs

These people are the great manipulators and so spotting them isn't always easy. However, because they are great plotters they can often be seen stirring the pot or twisting people to do their bidding through sneaky tactics.

The office gossip, usually spreading rumors and trying to get people to do what she wants – probably a high mach.

The quiet guy at a competition whispering to his teammates and pointing at other players – probably a high mach.

How to approach these people.

High Machs thrive on deceit and subterfuge so the simple way to beat them at this game is to be incredibly direct and show dominance. Don't try to play them at their own game – they will win. Instead, avoid any of their tactics or tricks and simply go for your goal.

In the office environment, this could be approaching the office gossip and openly confronting him/her about the false rumors and manipulation. Be confident and calm.

In the sports environment, go straight up to the guy making his plans and simply smile while asking how his tactics are working.

In both these situations, the sudden direct approach will usually cause the High Mach personality to shrink away, avoiding direct conflict where possible; ultimately giving you control of the situation.

Exercise: Test Your Ability to Spot Personality Types.

Next time you go to a public place and a have a few minutes to spare, calm your thoughts and take a look around at the people you see, ultimately trying to figure out what personality type they might be. Remember that some people may exhibit traits of multiple types, but one will usually be dominant.

1. Find a coffee shop, café or public space
2. Relax your mind and take a look at the people around you
3. Particularly focus on groups or pairs of people to see how they interact
4. Is one dominating? Is another scheming?
5. In your journal or on a scrap of paper, identify what you see, what personality type you think they are and most importantly, why.
6. Once you made your assessment, observe if their behavior continues in the way you thought. If not, why not?
7. To make it more fun, play the game with a friend, taking turns to guess at people around you.

HOW YOU CAN 'PSYCH-OUT' AN OPPONENT

Let's address the most common question concerning sports psychology. How do I "psych out" an opponent?

While this term has many different meanings, the most common application in people's minds is the ability to use your mental powers to instil fear and terror in the mind of an opponent prior to engaging them in some form of competition. Perhaps most famously, this has been used in boxing and combat sports to successfully intimidate an opponent even before the event has even begun.

Fights are not just physical conflicts – regardless of the sport or event involved. Beneath the blows and blocks, movements and throws, there is a silent battle of wills. Any form of boxing, or martial arts especially, is going to challenge your fortitude and strength of character in a direct contest. The movements you spent months trying to perfect will prove worthless if you allow your opponent to rattle your mind.

According to black belt and professional applied sports psychologist Dr. Alan Goldberg, success relies on both physical conditioning and Mental Combat training. Mental Combat training will allow you to turn the tables by establishing a formidable presence to psych out your competitor.

In order to dominate any match-up, you will ultimately need to show your opponent that you are unfazed by their intimidation tactics. You will need to control your emotions and hide your reactions. React with skill rather than emotions. Nothing will make your competitor feel more uneasy.

Martial arts, for example, is physical, but it is also personal and emotional. When you are matched against fighters who are well-trained, you will need to use every trick in your arsenal. This means both physical and psychological warfare. Rattling your opponents' mind will loosen their confidence and sabotage their game plan. The key is to do this without distracting yourself away from the fight. You need to maintain physical control and focus while throwing the other player off balance.

It is impossible for two fighters to be perfectly or evenly matched. When two people meet, one will naturally assume the dominant position. By approaching the fight with the right attitude, you can immediately psych out your opponent and establish a dominant presence. Without saying a word, or making a single movement, your stance and mental control can instill a feeling of inferiority in your opponent. This feeling can actually make their actions slower, less confident and less effective.

This doesn't just happen in fighting. It occurs in every form of competition. In the chess community, Bobby Fischer is considered one of the most respected champions. He had impressive skills and a prodigal knowledge of the game. These proved helpful, but the real key to his success is something that U.S. grandmaster Robert Byrne coined the term "Fischer Fear". Because Fischer was seen as such a talented player, his opponents regularly second-guessed themselves. This assumption of inferiority ruined their chances of winning. The fear physically manifested in the form of cold sweats, headaches, shaking and rising blood pressure rates. It is impossible to count the number of games Fischer won purely because he psyched out his opponents, but it had to be more than a few.

Researchers at Northwestern University refer to this phenomenon as the "superstar effect". They have conducted a lot of research on this subject, particularly pertaining to golf. Golf was carefully chosen because the only way that the players can affect one another's games is on a psychological level. One such study regarding Tiger Woods audited scores in various tournaments. The results showed that fellow golfers perform more poorly when Woods is present. They required an average of 0.8 more strokes than when he was absent. Those highest on the leader board, and therefore most likely to directly encounter Woods, were found to experience the largest effect. This is a big impact when you consider that most of these professional tournaments were decided by the margin of a single swing.

You may not have the fame or notoriety of Tiger Woods or Bobby Fischer, but you can still use Mental Combat training to psych out your opponents. According to research conducted by the American Psychological Association, your self-image is largely decided by external factors. You can use this knowledge to your advantage. There are techniques you can use to make your opponent question their own skills. If you act as though you fear them, they will feel more confident. However, if you ignore them, making their actions seem inconsequential, you can destroy their confidence.

Martial artists and boxers can manipulate their opponents both mentally and physically. In addition to overpowering them with strength, skill, and speed, you can rouse their nerves. Doing this will not only make them less effective, but it will also allow you to conserve energy and plan your next move more effectively. When this technique is mastered, it can significantly improve your chances of victory. Use the following steps to establish dominance and psych out your opponent.

1. Recognize that your words, actions, and body language can directly affect your opponent. Not all of your power comes from your fists. Your opponent will subconsciously respond in relation to how they are treated.

2. Never show fear. Stay composed and confident, even if they are

inflicting pain or discomfort. They will feel weak if you show that they cannot affect you.

3. Stand tall. Remain aware of the body language you are emitting. Walk slowly and confidentially towards your opponent. Act like you know what you are doing.

4. Never cower or hunch your shoulders. Defend your position without assuming a defensive demeanor. Do not act submissive.

5. Be quiet. Let them guess what you are thinking.

6. Hide your emotions. Do not shout, cheer, swear, cry or complain. Do not get angry.

7. Set your own pace whenever possible. Don't let your opponent lead or make you rush. Make them wait a little, but not excessively. You do not want to aggravate them.

8. Shake off errors. Do not react when you make a mistake. Continue on as though nothing happened. In fact, you might even choose to repeat the action to show that you have nothing to fear.

Nothing is quite as frightening as facing an opponent who makes quiet, controlled and purposeful movements. One never knows what they are thinking, or what they are capable of planning next. Creating a calm and intimidating presence can affect even the most experienced opponents. They may be physically bigger or better, but your Mental Combat training can provide a significant edge.

Apply these skills to improve your athletic performance and to manipulate the outcome of intimidating social or business interactions. Next time you want to ask for a raise do it in a calm, confident and controlled manner. Your boss will have no choice but to take you seriously.

Exercise: Practice Psyching Out Others.

Firstly, it's important to understand that there is a big difference between psyching opponents out and being a bully. We use the techniques of assertiveness and psyching-out to command respect, not to aggressively target vulnerable individuals. Now we have that out of the way, here's a simple game you can play to test your ability to psych out others and your projection of confidence.

1. Next time you are on the street, look for a pathway with a fair amount of oncoming foot traffic.
2. Move into the oncoming lane and, giving the people coming toward you plenty of time, aim to make them move to the side, rather than you move.
3. Draw yourself to your full height and fix the oncoming person with a steady, but firm look.
4. Keep your head up high and shoulders pushed back.
5. Move with intention and decisiveness, but not aggression – this is a tricky thing to master
6. Show no emotion or anger, simply try to urge your oncoming opponent to move through your actions and body language
7. If they move aside to let you pass, you win. If not, try again.

Note: With many people spending so long looking at a phone these days, it's important the oncoming pedestrian sees and engages you to avoid any shoulder barges.

HOW TO GENERATE CONFIDENCE

Confidence is one of the marks of a true fighter. It is something that radiates from all of the greatest athletes. It is an invisible entity which drives martial artists, boxers, and coaches to forge ahead, conquering new obstacles and breaking new records. You know when your confidence soars because you feel ready and excited to compete. You perform at the top of your game, without stopping to doubt your skills or decisions. The trouble with confidence is that it takes real effort to grow and it is also easily broken. Failed competitions, jealous teammates, discouraging parents and ineffective coaches can stifle self-esteem in mere moments. Without intervention, it can take a lifetime to recover.

In many cases, confidence is the thing that separates triumphant victory from miserable defeat. Research at Utah State University has confirmed that the confidence level of coaches and athletes plays a big role in the success of a team. They also found that the confidence level of the athletes is connected to their coach's confidence level.

Confidence is the thing that motivates you to take a chance, despite the risks of failing. An article recently published in the *Journal of Personality and Social Psychology* found that confident people perform better on tests. When you are confident, you perform better than your best. When your confidence is broken, you perform beneath your own abilities. Small mistakes become big burdens to overcome. You begin to stand in your own way. No amount of physical training can overcome a lack of confidence. The only thing that can overcome poor self-esteem is careful Mental Combat training.

The earliest definitions of confidence were written in terms of motivation. Athletes with high confidence levels are motivated and expected to do well. They are therefore more confident in aiming for higher goals. Confident players rely on themselves to achieve success. Efficacy, self-esteem, motivation, and confidence all go hand in hand. High levels of one of these qualities will stimulate a larger presence of the others. Together they will lead a dedicated fighter to success.

If you are struggling to succeed, then it is worth taking some time to evaluate your self-esteem. Do you regularly doubt your skills? Do you feel like you lack something that other competitors possess? Do you hesitate to strike out?

Do you feel intimidated by your opposition? You will never excel as long as you are distracting yourself with doubts.

Sports psychologist Dr. Costas Karageorghis has spent years studying the best ways to encourage athletic confidence. He believes that it is possible to grow your own confidence. Sports psychology has delivered a host of growing techniques to choose from. Figuring out how to boost confidence levels can take some experimentation. While some techniques are clearly more helpful than others, individual differences will cause athletes to respond differently. It will take a variety of confidence building techniques to effectively train an entire team. The best way to see if a technique is working is to question the participant. Coaches should be flexible and willing to try new Mental Combat training techniques when old strategies fail. Trainers and learners should work together to find the best approach.

It is easy to get started. Use these tips to build a wall of self-confidence. When you have a solid base of self-esteem, all of your physical training will come together more smoothly. Regularly use Mental Combat training to gain confidence and stop getting in your own way. These tips can be utilized by boxers, martial artists, coaches and trainers alike.

- Start with a few moments of self-evaluation. Confidence has to come from within. Think about the types of training that have worked well in the past. If you are sensitive in nature, choose a gentler approach. If you need tough love, then use a stern inner voice.
- Sit down and brainstorm some of your best skills or characteristics. Write these down on paper for now. Are you particularly strong, quick, motivated or efficient? Once you have a few good ones, make an effort to regularly remind yourself that these positive attributes exist. When you are matched with an opponent, recognize the areas where your skills match or exceed theirs.
- Fake it until you make it. Think of someone that you consider highly self-confident. Mimic their mannerisms and stance. (We have covered this one earlier.)
- Watch for negative self-talk. You need to respect yourself. If you have a habit of berating yourself, work on shutting off that voice and replacing it with a more supportive one.

- Be generous with positive feedback. When you or your student has executed something well, acknowledge it through praise.
- Instead of beating yourself up when you fail, take an objective look at what went wrong. Don't waste time being negative. Instead, strategize how you could improve your performance next time. Also, take time to recognize something that you did well despite the poor outcome.
- Don't set yourself up for failure. It is good to have lofty goals, but you cannot reach them all at once. In order to climb the ladder, you have to master one rung at a time. Make reasonable, attainable goals. This may mean entering a competition at a lower level, or focusing on landing three solid jabs, or winning one round, rather than winning the entire competition.
- Visualize success. Keep a clear picture of winning in your mind. This can be a proud moment from the past, or an image you plan on making a reality. Expect to succeed.
- Practice with dedication and work hard to attain physical skills.

Being confident takes practice. Success would come easily if this was a simple matter of telling yourself to be confident. In reality, you will need to repeatedly use a variety of techniques in order to instill a greater sense of esteem. It is not uncommon for athletes to experience inner battles regarding their skill levels. Fortunately, in this match, you know your opponent intimately.

The techniques described above can help you conquer your insecurities in addition to obtaining a competitive edge in your next performance. When you walk with confidence, there is no limit to the places you can go. Start building your confidence right now by listing three things at which you excel.

THREE TRICKS TO NEGOTIATE LIKE PRO

How to get the best deal in life.

I've been lucky enough to travel to many locations around the world on my travels and one of the things that frequently surprises me every time is just how bad we, as westerners, are at negotiating. If you visit Asia, the middle east or many parts of Africa, haggling for a better deal at the market is a way of life. It's not just expected, it's actually a part of the custom there and in many cases, it's almost an insult if you don't even try.

The fact is if we are skilled at negotiation we can get a much better deal out of life. Whether it is bartering for goods at the Grand Bazaar, getting yourself a pay rise at work, or grabbing the best price at a car dealership. It's not always about money either. The ability to read a situation, understand and stand up for yourself in negotiations is a powerful skill.

If you are confident and tenacious with your skills, you instantly gain respect and that can go a long way in life. Even if you aren't interested in creating a better first impression or changing how people see you, it's certainly nice to get thousands off the price of a car or get yourself a better salary.

Today, I'm going to reveal three powerful psychology techniques that have not only worked for me but thousands of other people around the world. The best part is that these tactics are proven to work, but largely unknown by the wider world. Which means the chances of it working are even better!

Let's go.

1. Knowledge

They say knowledge is power and in the negotiation game, this is absolutely true. The first step to getting a better deal in life is to know the market and the true value of things. This doesn't mean scouring the stocks and shares indexes or becoming some expert in commodities trading. It simply means that before you enter some kind of negotiation you already know roughly how much others are paying for the same thing and if there is room for movement on the price. Clue: There usually is.

1. Spend ten minutes looking online at prices and understanding the market
2. Understand mitigating factors like condition, age, availability
3. Decide how much a fair price is, and how much you should really pay.

4. Set a maximum price and be prepared to walk away after that

This tip also applies to things like salary negotiations. In another life, when I worked full-time in an office, I discovered I was being paid a couple thousand less than the market standard. I discussed this in a confident yet polite manner during my next review and sure enough, a raise was on the cards.

This works great for new jobs too. If you are offered a position, do your research beforehand and be prepared with evidence to prove why you should be paid more.

2. The Flinch

This is a sneaky, but very powerful psychological technique which plays upon human nature and the way we don't like to disappoint others. The basic principle is that deep down we all understand body language even more than words and we don't like seeing negative body language in others. This method utilizes that notion to your advantage by forcing your opponent (in the negotiation) to give a little in their approach.

The flinch is a reaction you make to show your distaste at the offer presented. You don't say anything, and we'll explore why in a minute, but you show an actual physical flinch at the price or the terms on offer.

This flinch can be a frown, a grimace, a shake of the head or an actual flinch, a recoil. The important thing is that it's clear you've had a bad reaction to what the other person suggested.

Let's use buying a second-hand car as an example again.

1. You do your research in advance and know the price you would like to pay. It must be a good deal, but realistic.
2. You talk to the sales assistant and he gives you the vehicle list price, higher than you wanted.
3. You show the flinch. You frown and suck a breath in surprise at the price on offer, but you say nothing and keep looking at the car.
4. The sales assistant, feeling uncomfortable with your reaction wants to keep you on his side, so he immediately begins bringing the price down. Or he offers some bonuses. Or he qualifies the price by saying he can speak to the manager to bring it down a bit.

Feeling bad for disappointing you, many people will do anything they can to get you re-engaged. This is especially true in retail environments, where customer relationships are key.

Just be careful not to overdo it with the flinch. A grimace and a sigh work well, but breaking out your amateur dramatics and pretending to pass out on the floor does not. The reaction has to seem genuine and believable.

3. Silence.

The final tactic is another sneaky one that flows perfectly from the Flinch. In fact, it should perhaps be called 'The Flinch and Silence.' Essentially, we are adding to the discomfort of the other person with this method and pushing them to a point where they start negotiation with themselves.

At the end of this, you will often find a significantly better offer than you started with without even saying a thing!

Essentially the idea is that much like the flinch, other people don't like awkward silences and will often do anything they can to fill them. That includes; lowering prices, increasing salaries, agreeing to different terms and even helping you out.

Let's go back to our car dealership:

1. You've done your research
2. You've been given a price you don't like
3. You flinch, show distaste at the price.
4. Now you maintain intermittent eye contact with the car and the salesperson but say **nothing.** Be strong.
5. After a few seconds of silence, the salesperson will now be very keen to break the gap and start offering better terms. Let him/her talk.
6. Here, you can re-engage them, or if you want, throw them a few more disappointed looks, glance back to the car a few times and let them keep negotiating with themselves.
7. Once you are confident they won't lower the price any more, or you have something close to what you want. Then YOU start negotiating yourself.

These three tips combined are incredibly effective and mean that before you even start talking about terms yourself, the seller or the other person has often already given you much of what you wanted, enabling you to start from a position of much more power as a consumer.

As a final note. Understand that skilled salespersons or negotiators will sometimes have training and the ability to use these techniques against you, putting the ball in your court, until you blurt out that you will take any old deal.

Don't let them use you in this regard. Stay strong, be an empowered negotiator. Don't feel forced to speak and if possible, look for a younger, less experienced salesperson who will be less likely to know these tricks.

Now go negotiate your way to a better deal in life!

HOW TO MEDITATE ON THE SPOT

Meditation is an incredibly powerful tool for not only calming and focusing the mind but also for improving the body through enhanced mental conditioning. The irony, however, is that most people think meditation is a complex and stressful thing to learn or that it requires years of training and the mental fortitude of a celibate monk.

This is, of course, simply not true.

Yes, some people dedicate their lives to the study and practice of meditating. These people can achieve some truly remarkable results. Nonetheless, you don't have to be a Zen master halfway up a mountain to see quick and effective results.

I wanted to include an excerpt from my bestselling book "How to Meditate in 2 Minutes" since it has helped so many people.

https://getbook.at/HowtoMeditate

I'd definitely recommend grabbing a copy if you are interested in learning effective meditation quickly with a simple step-by-step guide.

For now, let's take a quick look at the process of realistic meditation for you and me.

HOW TO MEDITATE IN 2 MINUTES

Meditation is always a personal experience and you are encouraged to approach it in whatever way is most comfortable to you. After reading through this guide you may find that some techniques resonate more than others, which is to be expected.

Once you have a preferred method, you can incorporate this into your daily practice or regular schedule. Before you get to that point, you may wish to begin with the most simple of the approaches: 2 *Minute Breathing*.

Focused breathing forms the basis for the majority of all Meditation and Mindfulness exercises. If you can perfect this, you can easily move onto longer durations or other techniques.

The following breaks the process down into 30-second segments to further aid in structuring your approach. As always, this is just a guide that can be modified as you see fit:

0-30 Seconds

- **Becoming Quiet and Still**

To start, your body and mind may be unsettled as you enter into the meditation. Use this first 30 seconds to become still and calm in both. Focus on staying in one position (of your choice) and slowing your thoughts. You may close your eyes to aid the process.

30-60 Seconds

- **Focus on the Breath**

Next, draw your attention to your breathing. Begin inhaling through your nose and out through your mouth. Focus fully on each breath and inhale for a mental count of 5. Hold for a count of 2. Exhale for a count of 5. Then repeat.

60-90 Seconds

- **Expand Your Awareness**

Now allow your thoughts to expand and fully acknowledge your own body and all of its sensations. Don't judge or try to change anything. Allow your mind to be free of concern and become loosely aware of how that feels.

90-120 Seconds

- **Combine and Close**

With all the previous parts combined: stillness, focused breathing and a relaxed expanded awareness, you should find a sense of calm and yet alertness, focused and yet thought-free.

It is at this point where all the elements coalesce that you find the most power. It is a kind of therapeutic trance state which is almost impossible to put into words. (And it feels completely unique for you so you don't need to try!)

Finally, as the time draws to a close take some deeper breaths and draw your attention to the ground, chair or cushion on which you sit. Feel and listen for your physical surroundings and when you are ready, open your eyes.

Don't Worry if it Doesn't Happen Right Away

The process above is the ideal way a brief two-minute meditation will play out. If it doesn't happen that way for you, there is nothing to worry about.

It's very common for the process to be as different as the individual practicing it. Simply use each 30-second strategy as a guide. If you find your thoughts wandering, bring them back in line.

Eventually, you will find the process becomes second nature and you won't even need to think about it. The same approach can also be applied to longer sessions in the same way but for different durations.

Exercise: Two-Minute Meditation

1. Find a quiet space and somewhere to sit. Don't try any complicated yoga poses or weird stances. Just whatever feels comfortable, but no crossed arms or legs.

2. Start a timer on your phone or watch.
3. Close your eyes and take a deep breath. Adjust your body for maximum comfort and try to become as still as possible as you exhale.
4. Now take more deep breaths in and out. Perhaps try a count of four in, hold for two, then out for four.
5. After three repetitions of this, breathe normally and just become aware of your body and any noises around you . Don't judge, just be aware.
6. Finally, as the timer comes to a close. Take a couple more deep breaths before returning your attention to the room and starting to gently move your fingers, toes, and limbs.
7. Repeat each morning or night. Routine is key.

IMPROVE YOUR CONCENTRATION

When you watch a martial artist perform, your attention is usually on the physical movements. Their techniques appear smooth, intuitive and almost effortless. In reality, a great deal of work is going on inside their minds. Martial arts require a huge amount of concentration. Esteemed sports psychologist Alan Goldberg theorized that in order to reach their full potential, an athlete must be able to operate the mind and body together. Martial artists require not just physical skills and agility but also a great deal of focus.

Sports psychology research demonstrates that, in order to perform at their best, athletes must attain the right state of mind. Studies evaluated by the Harvard Medical School confirmed that athletes who engage in concentration training to improve their focus gain a greater competitive edge than peers who dedicate the same amount of time to additional physical training.

In order to perform well, you must remember and utilize countless techniques at the right moment, in the right place, with the right strength and speed. In competitions, you must pay attention to your opponent and be prepared to make use of any sudden opportunity. However, you also have to be sure the location you choose is one that counts. At the same time, you must try to remember which off-limits spots to avoid.

You have to breathe and focus your energy. In martial arts, concentration often becomes energy, transforming into impressive speed and strength. While body conditioning has a place in martial arts, most practitioners do not rely on bulk or muscle alone. Careful, thoughtful movements controlled by mental training and concentration build the martial artist's real strength.

It is not uncommon for instructors of martial arts, such as karate, taekwondo, or tai chi, to give themselves entirely to their practice. The best fighters are able to concentrate so deeply that they ignore their surroundings, block out any noises, and become the movements. This deep concentration is sometimes called "being in the zone". While most athletes experience this sensation during game time, the deep concentration practiced by martial artists is a bit different. In sports, athletes often say they feel as though everything beyond the playing field seems to vanish for a time.

Martial artists are fighters. They must be prepared for anything, so their awareness of their surroundings is not gone completely, they still know what is happening around them, yet they consciously choose to concentrate on what is in front of them.

This is particularly important when it comes time to compete. It is easy to concentrate in a quiet room. Applying those skills in a big room filled with family members, friends, coaches, opponents, and strangers is another thing altogether.

This is the same challenge faced by any athlete in any sport. You need to be prepared to put most of your attention on your performance. Distractions throw you off balance, creating an advantage for your competitor. When you get it right, time will almost stand still. You will notice every detail of your opponent, which means your movements will be more accurate and effective.

Most participants do not begin with a disciplined mind or body. This is something that must be learned and practiced, just like physical skills. The best martial arts trainers teach both the body and the mind. With dedicated practice, the thoughts, observations, and movements start to occur naturally.

Martial artists have an uncanny ability to concentrate on many things at once. They can focus on their opponents' stance, the strike they sense is about to happen, the direction to block or deflect, and the path of their next move. They see these things in a clear yet fluid picture. With practice, you will be able to focus on all of these things without getting overwhelmed.

This deep concentration can be applied throughout your life. Having such impressive focus can make it easier to juggle multiple projects at work, keep your cool in stressful situations, complete homework, or solve household problems. In fact, Mental Combat training is great preparation for new parents. It might even help you avoid friction in your relationships.

One of the most common complaints amongst couples is that one partner is too focused on a book or television show to hear what the other is trying to communicate. Wouldn't it be great if you could pay attention to both the game and your spouse? Honing your concentration skills can dissolve numerous everyday problems, resulting in a calmer, more balanced life.

If you want to be the victor in competitions, as well as at home, then you should use Mental Combat training to improve your concentration skills. Many of the world's top athletes agree that concentration is the single most valuable tool on the playing field. The tips below will improve your focus so you can develop intuitive speed, strength, and agility. Concentration is best developed through intentional, daily practice.

- When you first begin Mental Combat training to improve your concentration, choose a quiet place that is free of distractions. As you progress, you will want to exercise these techniques in areas with more and more distractions to test your focus.
- Become aware of yourself. Sit comfortably with your spine stretched up tall. Take a deep breath and exhale slowly. Relax your muscles and scan your body. For a few minutes, just sit, notice everything but change nothing.
- Evaluate your biggest distractions. Think about your performances in the past. Make a short list of the things that threatened your concentration the most. Was your coach shouting? Did the crowd

make you uneasy? Did you get frazzled when your opponent scored a point?

- Your list of distractions is also your list of obstacles to overcome. Knowing the enemy is half of the battle. Train your mind to see these distractions as reminders to get your head back in the game.
- To counter your list of distractions, make a list of the things that require your concentration.
- Limit the distractions that you can control. Get plenty of sleep and eat a healthy diet. Take care of work or relationship stressors right away. Your mind needs to stay on the game.
- Visualize the competition from a strictly concentrated perspective. In your mind, practice your attention on only the important details.
- Worry more about your own performance than your competitor's size, weight, reputation, or attitude.
- Don't wait until the big competition. Practice your concentration skills during your training. This will provide an opportunity to adjust your game plan where needed.
- Have a focused, pre-game ritual. Enter the competition with a quiet mind. Literally, take a few minutes alone in a quiet space where you can empty your mind of all distractions. When you re-enter the arena, keep your eyes and mind focused on your game plan.

In order to reach your full potential, you will need to concentrate. You can train your mind to focus on the important things and let go of the distracting details that get in the way. Improved focus can enhance nearly every facet of your life. With better concentration, you will be better able to learn new skills, excel at work, solve problems at home, and compete in athletic events.

Kineticist, K. Porter, found that an athlete's ability to concentrate was closely related to their motivation in regards to maintaining the skill. Concentration training must be repetitive, dedicated and consistent. By using a few simple training techniques, you can begin to improve your concentration right now. Take a few minutes to relax and try the visualization technique described above. When you have finished, make a commitment to work on your concentration skills every day.

PRE-EVENT TIPS

There is an old saying within the Military that *"Proper Preparation Prevents P*ss Poor Performance"*. This adage is not just macho posturing designed to keep soldiers in line. It's absolutely true. Front loading the work (doing a bit more work ahead of the task) not only gives you a distinct advantage when it's time to perform, but it also reduces the amount of work you need to put in overall. Rectifying mistakes is far more time and energy consuming than getting it right the first time.

The key is to not only train physically for an event but to consider how you will mentally set yourself up for success. Sounds like hard work? Well, luckily the simple act of taking the time to acknowledge your anxiety surrounding the task ahead can make a huge difference.

"Failing to prepare is preparing to fail."

Research conducted by the Ohio Center for Sports Psychology has determined that, while nearly all athletes experience pre-game jitters, those who participate in individual events suffer the most. The reason behind this heightened anxiety is the fact that individual athletes experience greater scrutiny and attention than those participating in group sports. Boxers, wrestlers, martial artists, tennis players, and golfers report intense pre-game anxiety. Of all individual athletes, those involved in contact sports report the greatest amount of nerves in the days leading up to a competition. This is not surprising. In addition to being closely observed, these athletes also have the highest risk of getting injured during their performance.

Unfortunately, when left unchecked, this anxiety can make them even more vulnerable. According to the Association of Martial Arts World Wide, nervous fighters have a tendency to hunch forward, make awkward movements, and assume defensive rather than offensive positions. This increases their odds of taking serious hits from their opponents.

Competing is a large part of most sports. While it does come with the risk of discomfort, and even pain, most participants report that the experience is memorable, worthwhile and beneficial to the advancement of their skills. Competing provides an incentive to improve your skills. In the days leading up to the event, you will need to prepare mentally and physically. Both of these aspects are equally vital to your success; neither should be neglected. Physical training is relatively straightforward. Below you will find more information that will assist your Mental Combat training in preparation for any of the challenges you face on the mat or in your everyday life.

PRE-EVENT 1: HOW TO STAY MOTIVATED

Do you find yourself skipping training sessions or performing below your capabilities? Do you quit early or sabotage your work with poor lifestyle decisions? Are you struggling to put 100% of your strength and attention to your goals? Is your effort equivalent to the height of your ambitions? If you aren't living up to your full potential, then it is time to examine your motivation.

Every achievement is driven by motivation. If you lack the ambition needed to advance, then all of the training in the world won't make a difference. Possessing confidence, focus, energy, and fortitude are not enough. You have to want to use and improve your skills. You need a reason to continue training. In short, you need a deep and conscious desire to succeed. Nothing else will provide the fire you need to develop the skills essential to realizing your ultimate goal. Motivation is essential. It can be the difference between dreaming and doing.

Motivation is a familiar word, but what is it really? In the most basic sense, motivation is your ability to begin and continue an action. It is a desire to begin doing something, like practicing and training in your sport. It is also the thing that makes you willing to wake up and continue training day after day. It is that thing that keeps you from quitting before you have reached your goal by mastering your skills or competing in the most esteemed competition.

Researchers have found that intrinsic motivation is more effective than that driven by social or egoistic desires. One study found that competitive athletes who were intrinsically motivated were more likely to develop effective strategies for overcoming challenges during competition. Athletes in the same study, who were classified as being extrinsically motivated, were less likely to be successful because they had a tendency to avoid challenges, rather than confronting or overcoming them.

A separate study involving British college-level participants also found that athletes with specific goals related to the development of specific skills were more likely to be highly motivated by personal drive. Those with social or egoistic goals focused more on winning than becoming more skilled. In short, they were less motivated to develop the skills needed to achieve their goals.

Reaching your full potential will require intrinsic motivation. Your level of motivation will have to be strong and ample to get you through the toughest parts of training. Everyone can get through the first few days. However, most skills will take months if not years to master. Your motivation will allow you to continue working despite discomfort, pain, tiredness or boredom.

This point in your training is called the "grind". The grind appears when the new and exciting aspects of training wear off. What you are left with is hard, repetitive work. This is the time when you will be most tempted to quit altogether. A study conducted at Georgetown University involved collegiate swimmers as well as professional rugby athletes. That research showed that motivation, or the extent to which an athlete cared about their sport, was a bigger factor than any physical attributes in determining whether a participant was able to push through the burnout phase. This is a valuable insight. Being able to push through the grind is what divides the top performers from those who will never realize their goals. Real training is hard. The secret to making it through the tough times is motivation.

Research shows that the athletes who are most likely to work through the grind are those who enjoy the process. They do not enjoy the grind in the sense that it is fun, but they do derive pride and pleasure from working towards their goal. They can see and feel the work taking place, despite the pain and sweat. You cannot hate or avoid the grind, you have to embrace it. In order to do that you have to be internally motivated.

There will always be something else you could be doing, perhaps something more enjoyable. However, with motivation, you will stay committed to your training. It can also help you adopt a healthier life. With the right motivation, you will make better relationship, sleep, work, school, and food choices.

In order to be successful, you have to put everything you have into achieving your goals. This means that you put every minute of your time, all of your effort, every ounce of energy and your full concentration into learning more and performing better.

If you are still struggling to find motivation, then it is time to step back and reevaluate your goals. Is this the right sport for you? Do you really want to accomplish greatness, or are you happy with your current performance level? It may be time to quit and find another hobby. Or, you might be content to practice at a stress-free, amateur level. These are both valid decisions, but there is a third option. If you really want to continue and you really want to meet your maximum potential, then you must prepare to dedicate everything you have. Find the inner fire that hungers for success.

Recognize that your performance can be seen as the sum of three components. One component includes all of your abilities, such as your mental, physical or technical skills. To a certain extent, these are things which you were born with. While you can certainly train to improve your capabilities, it will take a substantial amount of time. The skill level that you bring to your training is limited by what you already possess. This is not something you can control or change right away.

A second component involves the variables within a competition. The biggest aspect is the challenge presented by your opposition. You cannot control your opponent's strength or fighting style. You cannot change the weather, environment or location.

The third component is motivation. This is actually something that you can control right now. By finding a suitable source of motivation, you can improve the outcome of your performance. If tomorrow you were faced with an evenly matched opponent, the only thing that would separate you is motivation. The fighter with the greatest drive to win would have a huge competitive advantage. If you want to foster a similar advantage, use the steps below to develop intrinsic motivation.

Motivation Checklist

- Choose a long-term goal. Choose something exciting and personally rewarding. Psychological research by Avi Kaplan and Martin Maehr proves that setting goals is an effective strategy for maintaining motivation.

- Set short-term goals. These are the stepping stones you must master on your journey towards success. Focus on goals that improve your skills.
- Write your goals in a visible location. Revisit and adjust them every few months.
- When you hesitate to put all of your time and effort into your training, remind yourself what you are working towards.
- Visualize what success looks like to you. Remind yourself that hard work is required to make your vision become reality.
- Imagine the wealth of pride you will develop when your goal is achieved. Explore these feelings when you are struggling to push through the grind.
- Associate the toughest parts of your training with positive outcomes. Know why you are performing each task. Each drop of sweat is making you faster, stronger or more accurate.
- Find a training buddy. Surrounding yourself with people who have similar goals can improve your motivation. There are also immense benefits to having a partner who understands your sacrifices and why you are making them.

Strive to be your best by making your athletic goal the focus of your life. Constantly ask yourself what you can do to perform better or master a skill more fully. Before you go to bed at night, ask yourself what you can do better tomorrow. Know what your goal is and be willing to do everything you can to make it happen. Developing motivation is something only you can do. The most effective motivation comes from inside you; it is powered by pride and self-reliance. Your coach can present new techniques, but it is up to you to do the work. Are you willing to devote more time, energy and sweat?

Challenge yourself to put everything you have into your next training session.

PRE-EVENT 2: TRAIN EARLY

You may dread getting out of bed and going for a run or doing some training, but evidence shows that the morning is the very best time to exercise. Sure, it wakes your body up, shakes off any sluggishness from the night before and it means you are not tired from work or other activities. Research also indicates that those who exercise in the morning are more likely to stick with it.

Not only that, but morning activity was shown in an Appalachian State

University investigation to improve the sleep cycle the following night. A good night's sleep is key to successful weight loss and weight management.

Another factor to consider is that, if you get it out of the way early, you won't have the mental baggage of knowing you have to hit the gym or work out later, dragging you down all day. It is for this reason that psychologists have found people who get chores and less enjoyable tasks out of the way at the start of the day tend to have a better mood and increased motivation later in the day.

Best of all, a recent study by Brigham Young University also showed early indications that mild morning exercise reduces unwanted snacking by lowering appetite later in the day. Participants showed a lower neural response to food. This is perfect if you are trying to lower your sugar intake in the afternoon.

So schedule an early morning workout. By getting it done first, you eliminate the chance that obstacles will appear throughout the day, preventing you from following through with your fitness intentions. Many people intend to work out during their lunch break, or after work, only to find that there is no time left. Be careful not to fall into this fitness pit.

The characteristics which surround the morning also provide greater advantages. If you have windows in your workout space, then you can watch the sunrise during the fall and winter seasons. In summer or hot countries, the air will be cooler, allowing you to get active before the temperature really starts to heat up.

Once you are done with your workout, you can shower and get ready for work with the confidence that you began your day doing something great for your body. This will make you more likely to choose good choices throughout the day. Working out in the morning will also boost your metabolism for several hours. You will burn more calories throughout the day without any additional exercise.

If you don't work out in the mornings, try it for a week and see how much better you feel about your performance and your mood in general.

Morning Workouts the Easy Way

Need a quick tip for making early workouts that little bit easier?

Simply put your gym gear or workout clothing next to your bed. If they are comfortable, you can even sleep in them!

The small amount of resistance involved in sleepily rummaging around for gym clothes first thing in the morning is enough to put some people off from working out. However, if they are right next to you or, even better, you don't need to get changed at all, then that small amount of resistance is removed. You can head out straight away!

Anything you can do to encourage that morning workout will be well worth the effort. The gym is less likely to be crowded first thing in the morning. You will be free to use the equipment without waiting in line or feeling self-conscious. You can also take advantage of the natural early-morning testosterone peak. Plus, you will earn the benefit of feeling stronger, focused, and more confident afterward.

Going to bed prepared won't just encourage you to work out in the morning; it could actually improve your entire day. Also, consider moving your alarm clock further away so you won't be tempted to hit snooze. Continue reading to learn why morning workouts are king.

PRE EVENT 3: HOW TO HANDLE NERVES

As you approach the big competition, you may begin to feel an uncomfortable tightness in your stomach. You might develop a headache or your muscles might suddenly feel weak. These forms of physical discomfort are often attributed to nerves. If you are feeling anxious about an upcoming skirmish, then you are not alone. The truth is that all competitors feel this way. The most successful athletes have learned how to put this energy to good use by focusing it to fuel their pre-competition preparations.

Nerves can hit a competitor at any time. Some experience an increasing case in the weeks leading up to the event, while others are hit like a stack of bricks just moments before they are scheduled to fight. Feeling uneasy does not guarantee that you will fight poorly, as long as you can work past these emotions. Take Russian MMA fighter, Fedor Emelianenko, for example. In the fighting community, he is well known for his calm, controlled demeanor and fighting style. Many of his fans were surprised when he bravely admitted in an interview that even he gets very anxious before competitions.

Handling Nerves Technique 1: Visualization

The difference between Fedor Emelianenko and the clumsy fighters described in the introduction of this chapter is that he has developed techniques that allow him to control his reaction to those nerves. You can use similar techniques to relax your nerves, too. As people are individually different, you may need to experiment to determine the right strategy for you.

For example, most fighters do well when they take a moment of calm solitude before a competition. While this is an effective tool for quieting the mind and focusing your attention, it doesn't work for everyone. There are just as many athletes who prefer to warm up with a group of companions while listening to loud music. On separate training days, try each of these approaches and evaluate your performance to decide which style better suits your personality. Regardless of the style you choose, you should develop a ritual that you can use to prepare in the last minutes before a competition.

Visualization and meditation practices can be particularly effective. A series of deep breaths and muscle relaxation techniques can also help manage the fight-or-flight adrenaline. Be sure to practice the tricks for establishing dominance previously discussed in this book in addition to physically preparing to boost your confidence in your own skills.

It is important to meet your nerves head-on as soon as they appear. Do not wait for your mind to spin out of control before you take steps to reel it in. Don't give anxiety an opportunity to build momentum. Research published in *Psyched* magazine suggests that your brain has a tendency to favor negative emotions, such as fear or anxiety, which can leave you vulnerable to nervousness. Part of Mental Combat is pushing those negative thoughts aside so you can focus on the challenge.

Remind yourself that you are physically prepared for this competition. As long as you let your training lead the way, you will be able to perform at your best. Remember that your mental state is closely related to your physical performance. This means you can fight nerves not just with more productive thoughts but also by physically relaxing your body. Next time you are feeling nervous, try to harness that energy into physical power or speed. Teach yourself to interpret a racing heart or sweaty palms as excitement rather than fear.

Handling Nerves Technique 2: Mindful Breathing

Mindful breathing is perhaps the simplest method for practicing mindfulness, which as we've discovered is arguably the most powerful tool in mental preparation for any event.

Simply put, mindful breathing draws the attention of the practitioner completely to the inhalation and exhalation of breath while remaining as still and quiet as possible. It is also the easiest way to start developing mindfulness as a skill since following along with the count is something anyone can do.

1. To begin, try to find a quiet area where you will not be disturbed. (Mindful breathing can actually be performed in incredibly noisy and stressful places too, but as a beginner, you will prefer to learn the skill in the easiest setting.)
2. Sit or stand and consciously relax all parts of your body. Try to ensure no tension remains, other than that needed to keep you upright.
3. Start to deepen your breaths in and out. At first, don't focus on counting, just concentrate on making them deeper. Do this for around 30 seconds.
4. Next, begin to consciously count your in breath for a count of 4 seconds. Then hold it for 4 seconds. Then exhale for 4 seconds.
5. Really try to center yourself on the breath count.
6. Continue this exercise for 2 minutes. Then, gently bring your attention back to the room around you, the chair you are sitting on or the noises surrounding you.
7. 2 minutes is an excellent starting point, but as the exercise becomes easier you may wish to try out longer durations or challenge yourself to the same 2 minutes but in busy and distracting surroundings.

Mindful breathing is a powerful way to calm the body and mind and center your thoughts prior to a stressful event. Studies have shown those that practice mindfulness regularly are more focused and more alert, and less likely to suffer from high blood pressure or stress, on a daily basis.

Try it out for yourself and discover the power of mindful breathing.

PRE EVENT 4: HOW TO TRAIN (YOUR MIND)

You have to train your mind for success. The fighters who perform the best are the ones who are confident in their training, prepared to push themselves to their full potential, and who believe that they will win. This is sometimes referred to as the "champion attitude". Be warned that it is not necessary to be arrogant or condescending. Just have faith in your abilities and know that you stand a good chance of winning if you do your best.

In order to gain this attitude, you must train your mind for competition. Physically push yourself to complete exhaustion, then jump back up and do some more. Practice shaking off pain or defeat. Your coach can provide training in which your emotions are challenged. Practice being focused and continuing to fight despite the discomfort. Leave every training session standing tall. Do not hunch your shoulders and stumble away. Act as though your competitor is watching you. You must put on a confident attitude to avoid appearing vulnerable. Practice hiding your vulnerability.

Another technique you will need to practice is visualization. In your mind, picture a challenging battle in which you succeed. Seeing yourself win will help you succeed for real. Visualize the techniques you will use to overcome your opponent. Repetitive visualization will build confidence in yourself and your abilities. Be warned that visualizations work both ways. If you see the competition as a failure, you may sabotage the match before it begins. Stay confident.

Prepare to be in an unfamiliar environment. A multitude of studies, including a recent review published in *Current Directions in Psychological Science* journal by the Association for Psychological Science, show that athletes perform better at their home location. To say this another way, they are more likely to fail on the road. While their physical abilities remain the same no matter where they compete, being in a new place psychologically throws off their game. You can practice visualization techniques to overcome this problem. Visualize your journey to the competition. Look online or ask your coach for pictures of the location. If it is nearby, visit the location in person. Repeatedly visualize yourself being there. By game day it should be a familiar place.

You should also mentally prepare to confront your opponent. Training on your own is a great way to learn new skills. However, you also need to practice those skills on real-life opponents. Practice on your coach or a fellow student. Before you begin the match, take a minute to become familiar with everything about them. Observe how they stand, move and breathe. These are things you will need to be mindful of throughout the fight. Practice watching for cues that they are tired, hurt, distracted or unbalanced. These cues will provide opportunities for you to make a more effective move.

In martial arts, when you observe that your opponent is vulnerable, you should double your efforts. This type of mental punishment will often compel an opponent to quit. Practice tiring your opponent out to bring them to the point where one last attack will spell defeat.

Your training should be extremely challenging. Do not save your hardest fight for the competition. It is important to practice a winning attitude, not just on game day, but every time you train. Below you will find a review of the techniques you can use to condition your mind for success.

- Train every day to improve your skills, form, and confidence.
- Understand why you are nervous. Change the way you think of these feelings by associating them with excitement rather than fear.
- Harness your nervous energy into additional strength. Let it motivate you to fight harder.
- Develop a plan or a fighting strategy.
- Practice with a live opponent. Observe them closely so you can learn how to identify the right time to attack.

- Visualize yourself winning.
- Take care of personal issues when they arise. Do not bring emotional baggage to your competition.
- Familiarize yourself with the location of the competition.
- Bring an encouraging friend or family member who can cheer you on without being a distraction.
- Establish a pre-game ritual. Take a few minutes of quiet calm or listen to a specific tune. Empty your mind so you can focus on the competition.
- Practice deep breathing exercises to calm your mind and boost your concentration.
- In the days before the big competition, get plenty of rest and eat a nutritious diet. Fuel your body right to prevent distractions.
- Prepare for the possibility that you may not win. Reward yourself for your effort regardless of the result.

If you want to reach your full potential, training your body is not enough. You must also prepare your mind to focus, fight well and overcome nervousness. By knowing the obstacles ahead of time, you can learn to overcome them long before the competition. Get your body and mind on the right page. Write down a list of things you can start doing to psychologically prepare for your next match.

POWER WORDS

The first tool many use to get a correct headspace is the application of focus or power words. A great number of athletes and top performers use focus words, sometimes called mantras to align their thoughts and bring clarity to the mind.

You can mentally train your brain to instantly change your focus, as well as calm your anxiety, by repeating a word or combination of words that instill confidence and focus your concentration. Whenever you feel overwhelmed or your head isn't entirely centered on the task at hand, you can repeat your power word(s). Through repletion and by practicing this technique often, your word will become a powerful trigger to refocus your attention and quickly stop any negative or distracting thoughts.

What words do I use?

It may seem like an easy task to come up with 'good words'. But the task requires a little more thought.

Focus words are used to express your intention. In our case, we are concerned with focus words that will trigger centering and power your performance. Think of it as a concise and specific goal statement. Exactly what are you trying to accomplish in your performance? Choose a focus word or group of words that instill confidence. Think "I will" instead of "I want to".

.   .   .

No Negging.

Another thing you will want to avoid is anything that is negative. For example, avoid including the word "don't" even if the overall message is supportive of a good performance. For example, instead of "Don't give up" tell yourself to "Persevere." Or "Keep pushing".

Negative words are always negative, regardless of whether the context is positive. Those negative words can hang in your mind isolated, removed from the overall positive message, so try to avoid them. Always focus more on what you want to accomplish than on what mistakes you don't want to make. The more you think of something, the more likely you are to do it.

Choose words that feel and sound like the action you want to complete. Often the feelings and emotions attached to your focus word are more important than the words themselves. When you practice repeating them, you'll want to envision the drive you'll need when you are performing.

Exercise: Creating Power Words

Grab a piece of paper and a pen or your journal.

Close your eyes and imagine yourself in the position you would like to be. (This also gives you an intro to visualization explored in my other books.) Imagine yourself winning that tournament, being given that promotion or quitting that bad habit. Make it specific and real in your head. Put yourself in your ideal self.

Now open your eyes and jot down six words that describe the 'ideal you' in that vision.

Craft your focus words from a couple of these adjectives. Typically terms like confident, strong, and calm crop up, which is fine, but try to avoid things like 'wealthy' or 'awesome' since these are vaguer and have little to do with you as a person.

Try to craft three focus words or phrases and then knock them down to one. The one that means the most to you.

You can't use anyone else's focus words to get the job done. They have to be your own, personalized words that actually mean something to you. I like to stick to just one word: "awake", "center", or "breathe". My training partners and friends often prefer slightly longer statements such as "I am strong." Or, "Calm is within me." Use whatever works for you. Personally, I like them short, sweet, and to the point. The quicker you are able to recall and repeat your focus words, the quicker you can actually become centered.

Take some time experimenting with a variety of words to find what works for you. It may help to sit down and really think about what you want to accomplish, what you want to radiate, and what you need to work on most. The answers may lead you to the best personal focus words to accomplish the centering you need when anxiety strikes.

To briefly review, here is a list of the traits your selected focus words should have:
- Concise and specific
- Instills confidence
- Positive
- Short
- Easy to remember
- Personal
- Practiced

Remember, the more you practice, the more effective this will become.

- Repeat your focus word often, both in training and at home so that it becomes associated with the calm, focused energy you crave.
- Use the words when you are also successful and calm. Let your mind associate the words with the sensations of positivity

In addition to using these terms to calm and motivate, you can also use them to rebound after a mistake. Everyone makes mistakes, it's how we learn. Don't compound a small error by getting bent out of shape or losing your concentration. Instead, use your power word(s) to get back in the game quickly. (But take care not to use them too often when things go bad, to avoid negative association.)

DURING-EVENT TIPS

There are many mental training techniques that you can utilize during an event. For starters, you can utilize the concentration, motivation, confidence, and psych out techniques provided in previous chapters. According to respected Chinese Kung Fu expert, Alan Goldberg, you can use additional techniques to overcome two of the biggest performance obstacles. First, you must be able to overcome the initial adrenaline rush that surges at the beginning of the competition. Later, when the adrenaline has run out, you will need to focus and fight despite physical and emotional fatigue. In both of these scenarios, Mental Combat tricks will help you stay calm, focused and in control.

We will focus on these two main principles here because during an event the last thing you want is hundreds of complex principles you are trying to remember. It is far better to have done the work in advance (preparation) and then just focus on the task at hand. So, to keep it simple we are looking at handling adrenaline and managing exhaustion.

DURING-EVENT 1: HANDLING ADRENALINE

Adrenaline can be a performance booster or a performance killer. Part of the reason why the adrenaline surge is so intense is because it is a feeling that most people do not regularly encounter. In order to control your response to adrenaline, it is important to understand why it is being released. According to Mayo Clinic, adrenaline is part of your body's natural stress response. When your body senses that it may be in danger, adrenaline is used to stimulate a fight or flight response.

As the adrenaline surges, your body begins to feel different. Your heart will start to beat faster. Your breaths with quicken. Blood may drain from your face, making you appear pale. Your mouth might suddenly feel dry. Most people report feeling extremely tired or even dizzy. From an evolutionary perspective, these are beneficial adjustments which prepare your body to fight for your life. However, in a competition, they can distract your attention and sabotage your performance.

As you approach a competition with this adrenaline surge, you might even be tempted to run and hide. Do not run. You must compel yourself to stay and fight. If you have trained well, then you already have the tools that you need to succeed. You cannot necessarily control when your adrenaline begins to surge, but you can control your response. There are strategies you can apply during a competition to avoid the adrenaline rush, or at least put its effects to good use.

- Approach the competition with confidence to minimize your stress response. Preparation is key.
- Control your breath. Take slow and even breaths. This will send a message to your brain that you are safe and calm. In response, your brain will begin to scale back the amount of adrenaline released.
- Remind yourself to relax.
- Move around. Standing still when adrenaline is surging through your body allows it to build to a point where you feel like you are about to explode. Instead, walk around a little to shake off some of the excess energy.
- Put your adrenaline to work. You have probably heard of the incredible amounts of strength people have miraculously summoned during life-threatening events. Focus your adrenaline into strength and speed.
- Give in to your training. Focus all of your attention on what you will do next.

You can improve your performance by staying focused and making good use of the adrenaline rush. Find an opportunity to create an adrenaline rush during your training so that you can test your response. The more prepared you are, the better you will handle adrenaline during your competition.

DURING-EVENT 2: HANDLING EXHAUSTION

Now that you have learned how to weather through the adrenaline rush, you might start to wonder what to do once it wears out completely. At some point in the competition, you are bound to get fatigued. The problem with exhaustion is that it blurs your performance. It slows your thoughts, delays your reactions, sabotages your stance and weakens the strength of your blows. It also dampens all of your other Mental Combat skills.

Athletes should be wary of both physical and mental fatigue. These can occur separately or together. Physical fatigue happens when your body's metabolic reserves are expended. The result is an increase of lactic acid and a decrease of glycogen, or stored energy. As a result, your movements are weakened and restricted.

Physical fatigue will continue until you rest and replace your energy stores. Mental fatigue is a little different. It can last for a few moments or a few hours. It is the result of tired brain cells when your mind has been processing too much information. Breathing deeply, repeating cue words, refocusing and renewing your confidence can instantly shake off mental fatigue.

Research has verified that exhausted athletes begin to decrease the amount of effort they put into their performance, particularly if they feel like they do not have a good chance of winning. An interesting study by the *American Psychology Association* also found that the same factors that reduce performance motivation, including fatigue, also affect your cardiovascular system's effectiveness in making the adjustments needed to increase your strength. When you mentally give up because you are tired, your body also begins to slack off.

From this research, you can see that it is important to stay confident and optimistic, especially when you are exhausted. Part of being able to do that is preparation. You need to practice competing past your point of exhaustion. You should also show up to the competition well rested and full of the right fuel. The remainder is left to the Mental Combat techniques you employ to stay focused, maintain confidence, and push through the exhaustion.

You don't want a little exhaustion to ruin everything you have worked hard to achieve. So, what can you do if your energy runs out before the end of the match?

- If you are exhausted, then your opponent probably is too. Instead of allowing your performance to crumble, look for the right opportunity to land an effective blow.
- Put a confident game face on, there will be time to rest and recover later. Remind yourself of your goal.
- Stay hydrated. Drink water throughout the competition, this means every time you have an opportunity. You can alternate with a sports drink that has electrolytes and a little sugar for an energy boost. Loren Christensen and Wim Demeere, authors of *The Fighter's Body: An Owner's Manual*, warn that dehydration can begin to drain your energy after a mere 30 minutes of training. This can happen more quickly during an aggressive competition.
- Conserve your energy. Don't go all out in the beginning. Like runners, martial artists have to pace themselves. When you feel yourself getting tired, make fewer, more powerful and effective movements. Make sure every blow counts by choosing carefully and focusing all of your efforts.
- Cast off negative or pessimistic thoughts. You don't have the time or energy for this now. Shake them off and focus on your next move instead.
- Remember to breathe. Your brain and muscles use oxygen for fuel. Taking deep breaths will also keep your mind fresh and alert.
- Use a cue word to focus your energy and re-establish a positive, confident demeanor. Choose a word in advance and practice using

it. Every time you repeat this word you should immediately perk up and pay attention.

Fatigue and adrenaline can be huge sticking points for competitive athletes. Competition is mentally and physically draining. With a little practice, you can harness the initial surge of adrenaline into energy, motivation, and power. As the fight progresses, you should use techniques that energize your mind to fend off exhaustion. Make a plan before your next competition. Choose which techniques you will use to overcome these barriers so you can focus more of your attention on defeating your opponent.

POST-EVENT TIPS

The end of a competition is the perfect time for your Mental Combat skills to shine. Competitions are intensely emotional for participants, coaches and fans alike. All of your training has culminated into a single result. You will find yourself experiencing a unique mix of emotions. Being able to navigate this roller coaster is an important component of athletic training.

The difficult reality is that every player approaches a competition with the hopes of succeeding, but not everyone can win. Someone must lose, and sometimes that someone will be you. When this happens, you must be able to respond with maturity and grace. You also have to be able to move past a defeat. Research at the Leeds Metropolitan University that was recently published by the *Online Journal of Sports Psychology* shows that players who attribute their sports performance to their own self-worth are at an increased risk to experience depression and relationship problems.

In the event that you do win, you still must control your reaction. There is nothing wrong with feeling proud, or even ecstatic, but it is important to be a good sportsman. Learn to react with humility and empathy. There is responsibility in winning. You must demonstrate that you are worthy of the honor and respect you have earned. Let us explore how you can use Mental Combat training to cope with defeat or handle victory more professionally.

POST-EVENT 1: HOW TO HANDLE VICTORY

Competing is one of the ways that athletes evaluate the effectiveness of their training. While it is exciting to see your name at the top of the scoreboard, it is important to manage your success honorably. Athletes who display good manners, regardless of whether they win or lose, are said to possess good sportsmanship.

One of the biggest components of good sportsmanship is humility. Staying humble after a big win can be challenging, but it is important for two reasons. First, it shows your opponents that you deserve the spotlight. It is better to be respected than hated. No one likes a conceited show-off. Keep in mind that there will always be someone out there who is just a bit more polished. Winning doesn't mean that you are a better person; it just means you performed well. The only one you should really be trying to be better than is you. Focus more on breaking your own records than outperforming the competition.

Secondly, staying humble will prevent you from becoming complacent. No matter what you have accomplished, there will always be a higher level to achieve. There is no end to athletic training. Staying humble allows you to continue looking for a way to improve your skills. You can be proud of what you have accomplished, but never stop striving. Realize that at any moment your luck could change.

In fact, studies by the sport confidence researchers, Robin Vealey and M.A. Chase, suggest that athletes who become overconfident or complacent after repeated wins are more likely to see sharp declines in their performance. When you get too comfortable with winning, there is a tendency not to work as hard. This gives your competitors a huge advantage. If you feel like you don't have to try, you won't. Meanwhile, your opponents are working twice as hard to eke out a win. You have to stay motivated if you want to stay on top. When you remain humble, you continue to see ways to work and improve your skills.

Those who handle victory best do the following:

- Be gracious and humble. Be someone younger athletes can look up to.
- Regardless of whether you win or lose, you should always shake your opponent's hand. Try to compliment them on something they have down well.
- Be confident without being cocky. Earn your competitors' respect and they will enjoy seeing you win. There is no reason why competition cannot be friendly.
- Never gloat or rub a win in your opponent's face.
- Don't become complacent. Keep looking for ways to improve. Never stop training or striving.

- Stay focused. Once you have achieved one goal, find something a bit more challenging to reach for.
- Be grateful for the opportunity to perform.
- Recognize how much hard work was required to earn your success.

While everyone trains to win, not everyone defines winning the same way. It is important for coaches, boxers, martial artists and athletes to remember that winning or losing a competition is not a matter of life and death. Keep your athletic performance in perspective. Whether you are on the playing field, in the gym, at work, or at home, real success isn't found in winning a contest. Success is the fact that you have worked hard without giving up. Success is showing up and trying. In sports, and in life, the only true failures are those who don't try. By putting in the effort it takes to improve your skills, you are already winning. It may be time to rewrite your definition of success.

POST-EVENT 2: HOW TO COPE WITH DEFEAT

It is not always easy to accept a loss. Many athletes report feeling inadequate, cheated, sad, resentful, depressed and even angry. You put everything you had into your training, and yet it wasn't enough to win. Sometimes this is just the way things go. There is only so much you can do to control the results of a competition.

Nonetheless, coping with defeat doesn't always get better with experience. You will learn better coping skills, but the more advanced you become, the more dedicated you will be. Each blow may begin to seem increasingly personal. It is hard to shake off the disappointment.

Research indicates that professional athletes have a tendency to evaluate their self-worth according to their performance. This is a particularly dangerous habit that you should avoid at all costs. It can begin an ugly cycle of decreasing confidence and increasingly poor performance.

Losing will happen. In fact, losing is essential to becoming a better player. Losing challenges you to improve. It shows where you can do better. The beautiful part is that there is always another opportunity to train and try again. You never truly fail unless you refuse to grow, maintain your confidence, and learn from defeat.

When you lose, you have two choices. You can get angry, or swaddled in regret. You can cry and scream. You can be mad at yourself for not living up to your expectations. You can tear yourself to pieces and vow to never compete again.

Or, you can stand tall and move forward. There is pride to be found in trying. Remain composed and confident. Champions don't win every fight; they bounce back and fight harder and with more intensity. The best thing you can do is to take an objective look at your performance. Identify areas for improvement, but don't just search for failures. You should also identify what you did well.

In every failure, there is at least one small success. You may not have won, but maybe you executed one really great kick, or perhaps you stayed focused throughout the match. It doesn't matter if you lose ten matches in a row as long as you are learning and improving a bit each time. Learn everything you can and use that information to adjust your training for the next competition.

Use the following tips to cope with your next loss:

- Shake your opponent's hand. Congratulate them on a job well done, and mean it.
- Honestly assess what your opponent did better.
- Control your emotions until you leave the competition. Stand tall and act graciously.
- It is okay to be disappointed. When you get home, allow yourself a set amount of time for wallowing. Then focus on moving forward.
- Accept yourself. Recognize that defeat is part of the process.
- Identify what you did well. Honor these accomplishments.
- Remind yourself why you chose to compete.
- Make a list of things you can improve before your next competition.
- Foster renewed confidence in your abilities.

It is impractical to expect that you will always win. According to the laws of probability, you will sometimes have to deal with defeat. The key is to respond with grace. Act respectfully towards your opponent and thank your coach for the opportunity to test your skills. Take what you can learn and shake off the rest. By effectively dealing with a loss, you will improve your chance of winning in the future.

POST-EVENT 3: THE "TEST" APPROACH TO DEFEAT

One powerful way to manage a loss is to not see it as a loss at all.

The way your mind interprets the events of your life shapes your perception of them. Hence if you see each loss as a crushing defeat, your brain will eventually start casting self-doubt, negative thoughts and nerves prior to similar future events.

Instead, think of each defeat as a "test".

A scientist doesn't get distraught when an experiment produces unexpected results and you don't have to either. You were testing your fitness, you were testing your techniques or you were testing the way that your team performed together.

So it didn't work as planned. It's time to analyze: Why? How? What could you do differently to achieve the expected result? Go back to the drawing board. Adjust your training the way a scientist would shape a new hypothesis. With enough adjustments, you will eventually find extraordinary results.

Removing yourself from the emotional part of a loss is a powerful tool in recovering confidence and coming back even stronger than before – which is the ultimate aim. It's natural to feel disappointed with a defeat but really try to take a second and become scientific with your approach. Analyze the "test" and literally write down what you did well and what needs to change for next time.

This is the key to self-improvement. There are no failures, only *tests*.

POST-EVENT 4: SPEAKING AFTER THE EVENT

One of the surprising facets of high-pressure competition is that, upon completion of your part, you will usually find yourself being asked multiple questions regarding your performance.

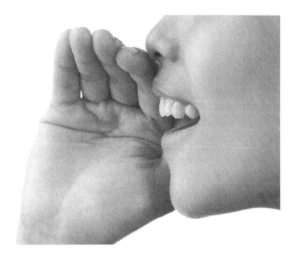

In the Martial Arts world, this could be theory testing following intense sparring or exercise, while in team events you may find fellow team-mates grilling you on what happened. This even applies to presentations within the office or work environment.

When the adrenaline is flowing it's tempting to blurt out a series of fast and unintelligible responses to get the questions out of the way.

However, a considered and careful response not only instills greater fear in any opponent but also inspires confidence in your team and yourself, so here are 2 very quick and easy guidelines to speaking at any high-pressure event;

1. **Slow down your speaking and any response. (The physical part is over, breathe.)**
2. **Pause. Take a full 2 seconds to think about what your reply will be and then say it. Count the 2 seconds in your head between each response.**

These tips may sound obvious but when the adrenaline is pumping and you are running on a high it can become difficult to concentrate on responses. The reason we only focus on two main aspects is because the brain is likely to forget the steps if there were more.

These simple methods involve slowing down response, breathing and becoming aware of what you are doing. This is an extension of mindfulness, which as we've discovered is a powerful tool.

PUTTING IT ALL TOGETHER IN AN EVENT PLAN

For most athletes, the key to success is being prepared. Part of preparing for a competition is devising a clear event plan. Having a plan that you can easily apply is far more effective than going with the flow. While many athletes devise plans of how they want to showcase their physical skills, psychological components are often left out.

Competition engages a multitude of Mental Combat skills. If you want to make use of them all, you have to arrive with that very intention. A study conducted by Robert J. Schinke and José L. da Costa at the University of Alberta and published in the *Athletic Insight: Online Journal of Sports Psychology* shows that Olympians with repeated success, referred to as reliant athletes, always approached the competition with clear tactical plans. If you are going to fight to win, you should be fighting on your own terms.

Simply going with the flow may seem easier. However, if you arrive with that mindset, you run the risk of being too pumped to follow through with any of the skills you have learned. Having an event plan means you can intentionally act, rather than simply reacting to your opponent. By not planning, you are already giving your opponent an advantage before the match even begins. In the moment, your mind may be too focused on what is happening to hatch a last-minute strategy.

Before you arrive, you should already know what attitude you will assume and how you will control the match. You should intend to use a variety of techniques to psych out your opponent so that you can gain the offensive advantage. Fighters with clear event plans tend to be less nervous and more motivated. Apply your confidence to create opportunities to exercise your most effective moves.

Boxing champion Joe Lewis attributed two things to his success. The first was having a plan. The second was having the willingness to adapt. You cannot just show up and hope to win. It is difficult to get where you want to go without a map. You have to plan on winning. This is your opportunity to bring all of your training together.

At the same time, you should expect your plan will evolve and strengthen as your experiences multiply. Do the best you can to start, and make adjustments according to what does and doesn't work for you. Eventually, you will be able to develop multiple plans. With time you will learn when to stick with your initial plan and when to switch to a backup. Often you will find that the holes in your physical skills plan can be filled with effective Mental Combat skills. Once you have your plan, you can use visualization techniques to practice seeing it through. If you can make and execute an effective Mental Combat event plan, you will become unstoppable.

- Empty your mind. Bring no baggage into the battle. Focus on the fight.
- Stay calm, confident, and relaxed. Walk and stand tall. Breathe

deeply. Keep a neutral expression on your face. Do not flinch or panic.

- Assert your dominance to psych out your opponent.
- Use your nerves. Harvest energy and motivation from the adrenaline rush.
- Develop physical defensive skills, but plan on being the aggressor. Even if you assume a defensive stance, never adopt a slouching, defensive demeanor.
- Acknowledge your physical weaknesses and decide how you can compensate.
- Be ready to adapt to your opponent's fighting style without becoming submissive.
- Use the first part of the match to analyze your opponent. Learn their size, strength, style, and weakness. Observe before making your first big move.
- In the second half, ration your energy. Pace yourself so you do not get tired as quickly as your opponent.
- Know when to push through the exhaustion and pain.
- Prepare to quit if you must. In fighting, quitting doesn't necessary mean failing. It means you are able to recognize when to choose survival. Choose a limit and stick to it.
- Don't plan on quitting. Plan to succeed.
- Display good sportsmanship. Accept the end result with grace.

Combine all of your Mental Combat skills to plan your attack. Know what techniques you will use to dominate your opponent. Know your limit, but do not plan on reaching that point. Plan to be confident, use your motivation, stay focused, and win. In the end, the biggest challenges in life and in athletics are the same. It is essential to know when to stay and fight, and when to walk away. Fight because you want to become better, not simply to be able to say that you won. Train with heart and bravery, not ego or conceit. Plan to learn and grow from every competition.

APPLYING MENTAL COMBAT TO EVERYDAY LIFE

The benefits of Mental Combat training can be applied outside of competitive events. Everyday life can be far more rewarding when you put your brain's new abilities to work. Don't just be a warrior on the court; maintain the same spirit in everything you do. This can improve the way you handle stress, manage relationships, function at work, spend your free time and approach your fears.

At home:

- Reducing stress (See Mindfulness chapter)
- Improving confidence
- Learning how to meditate for just 2 minutes a day

At work:

- Analyzing a rival's personality type (and using that knowledge)
- Improving concentration
- Increasing motivation

Out and About:

- Handling a sudden violent situation (Car crash or mugging)
- Getting your way when dealing with awkward people
- Conquering fears and panic

Numerous studies have provided evidence supporting the ability of these skills to create cognitive, behavioral, and effective benefits. It makes sense that skills which foster greater confidence would build self-esteem and assertiveness. You can use these skills to get what you want in life. People with greater confidence levels are also less likely to suffer from anxiety or depression. When you are mentally ready to face your fears head-on, you will be more likely to attain personal and financial success.

You encounter stress everywhere. Imagine how much better life would be if you approached life stress the same way you tackled an opponent in the ring. Applying concentration and good sportsmanship can also improve your interactions with others. Konzak and Boudreau found that this type of conditioning can make you less aggressive and impulsive. When you are calm and focused rather than agitated, you will be able to handle stress more appropriately.

Good sportsmanship can help you get along with others. Remember to pay attention not just to language, but to body language. Act respectfully and confidentially without being boastful or rude. This will lead to more positive social interactions both at work and in your personal life. When you put these skills to work, you will excel at social networking and sustain healthier relationships.

Being focused and disciplined can improve your performance outside the arena. A study printed in the *Journal of Applied Developmental Psychology* found that students who had been exposed to martial arts training scored better on math tests. Use your motivational training to obtain your personal goals. By being focused and motivated you can achieve any dream you wish to achieve.

Life is difficult. You may often feel challenged or tempted to give up because it is just too hard. Stop stressing and decide what you want. What is your motivation? Set a goal and do what you need to do to achieve it. Work may become more tolerable when you look at the bigger picture. The time you spend at work is an investment towards your goal. Just like in your athletic training, you can set attainable mini-goals to help you work towards a job promotion, larger house, or bigger savings account.

Adapt your life the same way you adapt your game plan to battle an opponent. Life comes with challenges. Sometimes you will need to fight through the exhaustion. At times you will take hits whether it be in the form of a lost job, divorce, illness, or death of a loved one. You can treat these blows the same way you treat them in a competition. You can absorb and accept them. You can learn the lessons and move forward stronger and more determined. When you score, share and celebrate your success with loved ones without being boastful or arrogant. Appreciate all of the opportunities you are given and keep striving to do better.

Use your Mental Combat training to manage the way you interact with the world. Establishing dominance in an unforgiving, fast-paced world takes mental fortitude. Life will not slow down for you; you must assert yourself to achieve your personal goals. The way you react to the people and challenges in your life decides whether you survive or thrive. Below is a list of ways you can apply Mental Combat training to everyday life;

- Be focused and motivated. Set a goal that you are willing to work for.
- Pay close attention to friends, family members, and enemies.
- Be confident and assertive. Do not let anyone take advantage of you.
- Use good manners.
- Stretch your mind.
- Know when to fight and when to walk away.

- Stay calm under pressure.
- Celebrate success.
- Accept loss or failure. Learn what you can to prevent future problems.
- Never stop striving.

The confidence and self-esteem derived from Mental Combat techniques can affect your entire life. Benefits can be experienced at home, in your relationships and in any activity you choose to participate. Mental Combat training will allow you to better handle even the most challenging interactions and boost your motivation at work. When you feel better about yourself and your performance, you will find one of life's most simple pleasures — happiness.

THANK YOU FOR READING

Thank you for reading. I've always found the psychology behind physical performance fascinating. In compiling this book, I wanted to share some of the incredible secrets of sports psychology that I have discovered over the years.

I hope you have discovered the real benefits that mental application can lend to physical performance and how, with a few simple exercises, you can not only boost confidence but reduce nerves, improve motivation and get the most out of sports, fitness or life!

Enjoyed this book? Please leave your review…

I work hard to create useful and easy to follow guides for Martial Arts, Fitness, Self Defense and well-being but I don't have a publisher's backing, like many authors. If you found this book interesting, please take 30 seconds to leave a quick review.

Positive feedback makes a world of difference to authors and other readers alike so please leave a review if you enjoyed reading.

- Phil

READY FOR MORE?

Discover the follow-up to Mental Combat in the acclaimed **INVINCIBLE MIND**: The Sports Psychology Tricks YOU can use to Build an Unbeatable Body and Mind!

http://getbook.at/InvincibleMind

Inside Invincible Mind, you'll discover:

- How to read any opponent using body language
- How to turn pain into power
- The secret method for mastering any skill in 30 days
- How to train for lightning reflexes
- Why ____Words can revolutionize your training
- The strategy for creating rock-solid positive habits
- How to manipulate an opponent (the right way)
- The mindfulness technique everyone should know
- And much more!

Get your copy now.

SELF DEFENCE MADE SIMPLE

**Self Defense Made Simple: Easy and Effective Self Protection
Whatever Your Age, Size or Skill!**
The No.1 Self Defense Bestseller!

http://getbook.at/SelfDefense

Discover 'Self Defense Made Simple' from Bestselling Self Defense Author
Phil Pierce: Your blueprint for smarter, easier and more intuitive self-protection without the years of training or complicated lessons!

How to Meditate in Just 2 Minutes: Easy Meditation for Beginners and Experts Alike!

The No.1 Meditation Download!

https://getbook.at/HowtoMeditate

Given, Meditation can be an incredibly powerful tool in improving both physical and mental health, focus and relaxation but most people think it takes a long time to see results. The truth is, it doesn't!

With this easy-to-use book, you can quickly learn how to achieve these incredible benefits in just 2 Minutes a day...

✵ Created with Vellum

Printed in Great Britain
by Amazon

15540046R00099